Greenwich Readers

Education & Training for Life

Perspectives
on Learning

This Reader is one of a series designed to support teachers and trainers in the post-compulsory sector of education. It will be of value to those who are working in colleges of further and higher education, sixth form colleges, adult and community education institutes, training units, and institutions of specific vocational preparation in the health service, the police service and the armed forces. The topics have been selected to represent a wide view of currently important issues and, by providing appropriate material for critical reflection on professional practice, the book will meet the needs of experienced teachers and trainers as well as those in the earlier stages of their careers.

In addition to such general use, the volume is one component of an integrated Certificate in Education/Postgraduate Certificate in Education course offered by the School of Post-Compulsory Education and Training at the University of Greenwich. Further information on this and other programmes of study and related academic services may be obtained from:

School of PCET
University of Greenwich
30 Park Row
London SE10 9LS

telephone: 020 8331 9230
fax: 020 8331 9235
e-mail: pcet@gre.ac.uk
www.gre.ac.uk

The planned range of titles in this series is as follows:

- Adult Learners, Key Skills & the Post-16 Curriculum
- Equality, Participation & Inclusive Learning
- Flexible Learning & ICT
- Language, Communication & Learning
- Perspectives on Learning
- Planning Teaching & Assessing Learning
- Professionalism, Policies & Values
- Supporting Students

Enquiries about the current availability of these publications should be addressed to the School Office at the above address.

Tony Lewis
Series Editor

Perspectives on Learning

A Reader

Michael Bloor
&
Ann Lahiff

Published in 2000 by Greenwich University Press and prepared for publication by:

Procurement and Business Services Department
University of Greenwich
Woolwich University Campus
Wellington Street
London
SE18 6PF

ISBN 1 86166 076 6

Cover designed by Pete Birkett

Text design and layout by Christine Murray

In the majority of cases the contents of the readings and extracts in this volume have been reproduced as they appear in the publications from which they have been taken.

Every effort has been made to trace all the copyright holders, but if any have inadvertently been overlooked the publishers will be pleased to make the necessary arrangements at the earliest opportunity.

University of Greenwich, a charity and a company limited by guarantee, registered in England (reg no 986729). Registered Office: 30 Park Row, Greenwich, London SE10 9LS.

Contents

Acknowledgements

Acknowledgement is made to the following for permission to reproduce the extracts and diagrams quoted:

Abbott P & Wallace C (1997) *An introduction to sociology: feminist perspectives* 2nd edn Routledge, pp85–90; 93–101

Bates I (1993) 'When I have my own studio...' in I Bates & G Riseborough *Youth and inequality* Open University Press, pp72–77

Biehler R & Snowman J *Psychology applied to teaching* 5th edn Copyright © 1986 by Houghton Mifflin Company, pp399–408; 422–431; 478–494 Reprinted with premission.

Bilton T (1996) 'Cultural deprivation' in T Bilton, K Bonnett, P Jones, D Skinner, M Stanworth & A Webster (1996) *Introductory sociology* 3rd edn Macmillan, pp352; 356

Clarke J (1997) 'Ethnicity and education revisited' *Sociology Review* 7 (2) November, pp32–33

Curzon LB (1997) *Teaching in further education: an outline of principles and practice* 5th edn Cassell, pp96–97; 102–106; 113–120; 209–228

Davies T (1994) 'Disabled by society?' *Sociology Review* 4 (4) April, pp15–19

Giddens A (1989) *Sociology* Polity Press, pp8–11

Giddens A (1997) *Sociology* 3rd edn Polity Press, pp18; 23–24; 212; 417–419

Hartley J (1998) *Learning and studying: a research perspective* Routledge, pp33–57

Hayes N (1993) *Principles of social psychology* Lawrence Erlbaum Associates, pp91–95; 99–101 Reprinted by permission of Psychology Press Limited

Kelly L (1992) 'Not in front of the children' in M Arnot & L Barton *Voicing concerns: sociological perspectives on contemporary education reforms* Triangle, pp31–32

Mac an Ghaill M (1989) 'Coming of age in 1980s England' *British Journal of Sociology of Education* (Taylor & Francis Ltd, PO Box 25, Abingdon, OX14 3UE) 10 (3), pp274–278

Marsh I, Keating M, Eyre A, Campbell R & McKenzie J (eds) (1996) *Making sense of society: an introduction to sociology* Longman, pp7; 464–470

McNeill P (1981) 'Language' in P McNeill & C Townley (1984) *Fundamentals of sociology* Hutchinson, pp116–118

Thanks also to Dr Chris Lloyd for permission to quote from the University of Greenwich 1998 handbook *Access to learning for students with disabilities*, p5.

The School of Post-Compulsory Education and Training

The School of PCET, as it is known, has its origin in Garnett College in London, one of three institutions set up by the Ministry of Education in the late 1940s for the initial training of technical college lecturers. After many developments and organisational changes over the past 50 years, its future within the University of Greenwich will now be from a campus on the banks of the River Thames in Christopher Wren's former Royal Naval College.

The School's services and students, though, are not only locally based, but nationwide and international. PCET is a leader in distance provision for lecturers, trainers, administrators and other support staff from all sectors of post-school provision, as well as from the public services and voluntary and commercial training organisations. It has associated centres in various parts of the United Kingdom, and there are projects in China, South Africa and Russia, and leadership of research and information networks within the European Union.

We aim, in both our teaching and our research, to relate professional practice to learning theory and current policy issues. This permeates all of the School's programmes – from initial training on Certificate in Education/PGCE programmes, through professional development at BA/BSc and Masters levels and the work of our Training and Development Office, to our portfolio of short courses and bespoke in-house provision. There is a thriving group of research students, and the School has been at the forefront of innovation in computer mediated communication. We provide a comprehensive service for further, higher and adult education, helping people to help others learn through life.

Ian McNay
Head of School

Michael Bloor is a Senior Lecturer in the School of PCET at the University of Greenwich, where he teaches Psychology and Education. His research interests include the accreditation of prior learning and theoretical issues in the acquisition of professional knowledge.

Ann Lahiff worked for a number of years in colleges of further education in London before joining Greenwich, where she is programme leader for the MA and MSc degrees in the School of PCET. Her principal teaching areas are the Sociology of Education, Equality Issues and Educational Research Methods. Her current research interests lie in the impact of computer mediated communication on teaching and learning and the development of CMC as a research tool.

Introduction

This Reader comprises a collection of articles, sections of books, and specially written materials that have been selected to provide an understanding of the processes of teaching and learning applied to the post-16 sector. The main theoretical approaches that we have used lie within the disciplines of the psychology and the sociology of education, each of which is concerned with the study of 'what people think and do as they teach and learn in a particular environment where education and training are intended to take place' (Berliner, 1992).

Teaching and training are not the simple, straightforward activities that some people imagine them to be; in fact they constitute one of the most complex of professional occupations (Rowan, 1994). To be informed and effective, a teacher needs to have both a wide knowledge base and an extensive range of skills. Porter & Brophy (1988) have developed one model of good teaching which suggests that a teacher's knowledge base should include:

- knowledge about the subject matter
- knowledge about teaching and learning
- knowledge about students.

Some teachers may feel that knowledge of their subject matter is the most important of the three; yet research suggests otherwise. Ferguson & Womack, quoted in Biehler & Snowman (1997), found that for students training to become secondary schoolteachers their grades in education courses were a better predictor of their subsequent effectiveness as teachers than grades in subject specialism courses. In fact the very rationale for the Reader is that effective teachers are those who have an understanding of the theory and practice of teaching and learning and can apply these ideas to the classroom.

The overall aim of this collection of commentaries and readings is thus to explore a variety of theoretical and research-based approaches which are relevant to post-school learning and to see how far teachers and trainers can apply these to their own teaching/training contexts. The text is arranged in three Parts, each covering a particular theme or set of issues in relation to models of teaching, the characteristics of learners, and the management of learning.

The first Part (*Teaching and Learning*) reviews a number of theories of learning and associated teaching strategies – including topics such as information-processing and memory – and offers guidance on how information can be effectively presented to students so that meaningful learning occurs and can be remembered over a period of time. There are substantial extracts from several writers dealing with the teaching and learning of physical skills, of higher order or cognitive skills, and of attitudes and behaviour.

Part Two (*Student Diversity*) begins by presenting contributions which consider how students are psychologically and culturally different from each other in terms of their approach to learning. It then goes on to explore issues of access, equality and diversity from a sociological perspective, with particular reference to examples such as race, gender, sexuality, social class and disability. The main emphasis is on how teachers and trainers can recognise, accommodate, and utilise these differences and achieve effective and supportive learning situations for all of their students.

The final Part (*Maintaining an Effective Learning Environment*) surveys some of the classroom management techniques which teachers can employ in dealing with issues of student behaviour. Selected theories of motivation and group management are directly applied to the improvement of a teacher's ability to establish a controlled and purposive context for learning.

Michael Bloor & Ann Lahiff
May 2000

References

Berliner D (1992) 'Telling the stories of educational psychology' *Educational Psychologist* 27 (2), pp143–161

Biehler R & Snowman J (1997) *Psychology applied to teaching* 5th edn Houghton-Mifflin

Porter AC & Brophy J (1988) 'Synthesis of research on good teaching' *Educational Leadership* 45 (8), pp74–85

Rowan B (1994) 'Comparing teacher's work with work in other occupations' *Educational Researcher* 23 (6), pp4–17

Part One – Teaching and Learning

This Part is concerned with aspects of how people learn and what actions teachers can take to promote the effective learning of their students or trainees. In order to help us do this, we make the familiar – if somewhat simplified – distinction between skills, knowledge and attitudes, and we explore in detail the role that memory plays in cognitive learning.

The first contribution concentrates on the acquisition and teaching of physical or 'psycho-motor' skills, that is those primarily involved in vocational areas such as engineering, building services, catering, beauty therapy and hairdressing. Some of the models of skill acquisition however – acknowledging the difficulty of determining exactly where we should draw the line – also cover the development of intellectual skills such as the demonstration of mathematical ability.

In the extracts which are reprinted in the second section LB Curzon considers what are often called the 'higher order' conceptual skills. He explores aspects of cognitive learning theory – that is, how we can go about achieving a meaningful, organised cognitive framework of facts, concepts and principles. He is concerned also with the importance of memory in learning, and analyses this in the context of learners as processors of information. According to Biehler & Snowman (1997) this information-processing view of learning is based on three major assumptions, each of which gives useful practical cues to the teacher in the planning of learning:

- Information is processed in a series of steps or stages. These involve attending to the information, recognising it, and encoding or transforming it into some type of mental representation.

- There are limits to the amount of information that can be processed without the learner becoming overloaded and inefficient.

- The human information processing system is interactive and dynamic, as previously learned information affects how and what people are currently learning.

There is therefore a close interaction between information processing, memory and learning. Being aware of some of the research in this area will help us to take this into account when we plan and deliver lessons to students and trainees.

Curzon then considers the process of cognition from two contrasting perspectives, that of David Ausubel and that of Jerome Bruner. Ausubel presents a strong argument for a teacher-centred approach (reception learning), while Bruner puts forward the case for more student-centred approaches (discovery learning). Each of these can offer useful strategies for teachers to consider.

1

In the planning of lessons there is a tendency for teachers to concentrate on the learning of skills and knowledge, and to believe that the confirmation or changing of attitudes is none of their business. However, very often the development or modification of attitudes is an important part of the learning. In the third section Nicky Hayes explores the function of attitudes in learning, together with some theories of attitude change.

Reference

Biehler R & Snowman J (1997) *Psychology applied to teaching* 5th edn Houghton-Mifflin

1.   The Acquisition and Teaching of Skills

Michael Bloor

In colleges and training organisations we hear the term 'skill' used in a variety of ways. In some areas of the curriculum we speak of 'core' or 'key' skills, which may include:

- social skills – such as co-operating with others
- language skills – such as reading, writing, listening and speaking
- number skills – such as measuring and calculating
- decision-making skills – such as problem solving and planning
- practical skills – such as manual dexterity and hand-eye co-ordination
- information technology skills.

The terms 'basic', 'core' or 'key' skills are used not because they necessarily refer to low-level skills but because they are considered fundamental to many jobs and encompass what are sometimes called 'social and life skills'. The terms may also include certain attitudes, knowledge and experience that employers require and value. Such an all-embracing use of the word 'skill' is problematic and raises important issues about where we draw the boundaries around it.

If you take one of the above examples – the use of speech, say – you will immediately see how complex the relationship is between the skill components (making the actual, recognisable sounds of the language), the knowledge components (understanding the difference between, for example, 'lie' and 'lay'), and the attitudinal components (wishing to use a language register that is appropriate for the listener/s).

In this section I shall concentrate on the more restricted, everyday use of the word and consider the acquisition and teaching of physical or 'psycho-motor' skills – as compared with knowledge ('cognitive skills') and attitudes ('social and behavioural skills').

Annett (1989) defines a skill as behaviour, with three characteristics:

1. it is goal directed;
2. it is organised so as to be reliably achieved with an economy of effort and time;
3. the behaviour has been acquired by training and practice.

Although Annett is here talking about physical skills it is clear that this definition could also be applied to cognitive and social skills.

A similar definition is provided by Fitts & Posner in their book *Human Performance* (1968):

A skill is a learned ability to bring about a predetermined result with maximum certainty and minimum time and effort.

Each of these definitions draws attention to the process of *learning* or *acquiring* the skill.

Models of skill acquisition

A. *The behaviouristic (stimulus-response) model*

Fitts & Posner have put forward a behaviouristic model of skill acquisition. This regards skill development as the forming of stimulus-response (S-R) links, so that the skill would be performed automatically given the right stimulus. They express this theory in terms of the following 3-phase model of skill acquisition:

1. *Cognitive* phase: the person learning the skill understands what is required and how to achieve the goal.

2. *Association* phase: the skill is practised to develop the necessary stimulus-response connections; feedback or reinforcement is essential for this to happen.

3. *Autonomous* phase: the skill becomes automatic and is performed almost unconsciously.

However, with the increase of the use of information and communications technology a new approach to skill acquisition has been developed.

B. *The information-processing model*

Theorists such as Welford (1976) have argued that a person behaves rather like a computer, receiving information, processing that information and producing an output of behaviour. Like the behaviouristic model it is concerned with input and output, but it places much more emphasis on the internal programmes – what is happening inside the person – as the skill is being acquired and performed. Hayes (1998) has proposed the following 5-component model of skill acquisition:

1. *Planning stage:* At this stage the person identifies what is required and develops a cognitive plan, schema or programme to guide their responses towards this goal.

2. *Perceptual organisation:* The person acquiring the skill begins to identify the sensory information which is relevant to the skill; other less crucial information is filtered out and ignored.

   Remember the first time you drove a car, sitting behind the wheel driving up to a busy street? There was a lot of information in front of you, from the street, the pavement, the car instrument panels and so on. At the start it was difficult to know what to attend to and what not to. Eventually though you soon acquired the appropriate perceptual organisation and the panic caused by the overload of information became manageable.

3. *Economy of motor action:* The person begins to learn to perform the motor or muscle responses effectively and efficiently.

4

So, referring again to learning to drive a car, you start to be able to balance the clutch and the accelerator and change gear smoothly without crashing the gears or moving the car jerkily.

4. *Timing:* Here the sub-tasks are gradually joined together to enable the person to perform the whole skill smoothly and effectively. Each subtask is fitted together into a continuous skill.

So not only can you change gear efficiently now – but you can do this at the same time as overtaking or taking avoiding action.

5. *Automatic execution:* The learned skill becomes almost unconscious. You do not have consciously to think and attend to the skill all the time.

Now, for example, you can drive to work or college and carry on a conversation with your passenger or listen to the radio.

C. *Skills as hierarchical schemata*

Annett (1989) suggests that skills are hierarchically organised programmes of motor actions or motor schemata. According to this model, acquiring skills involves the development of routines or units of motor responses which eventually become automatic. For example when we are learning to type, or to swim, or to drive a car, development does not happen from the beginning in a smooth and continuous manner, but we will improve steadily for a while and then reach a *plateau* or a stage where we practise and practise and for a time don't seem to improve. It is very important not to give up at this point; many of us will remember feeling that we would never get the hang of acquiring the motor skills of swimming or, indeed, motoring.

In typing, as another example, a person is slow at first while they become familiar with the position of the letters on the keyboard; as they learn these their typing speed will get faster and faster. Then typically they will reach a learning plateau as they begin to acquire the motor schemata for individual words, which they will then soon begin to type as a single unit. At this stage their speed will steadily increase with practice until they reach a learning plateau for phrases. And so on through the hierarchy of skills.

Stages of teaching practical skills

1. *Task analysis*

It is important to break a skill down into its component parts. This analysis of the sub-skills involved is useful for several reasons. Firstly, you will be able to identify more manageable units or sub-skills and prevent your students being overloaded with information. Secondly, as each student masters each sub-skill they will experience a feeling of confidence and progression. However, teaching this is not always an easy task for a highly skilled person. In fact, the more skilled you are at something, the more it has become an unconscious process, and the harder you may find it to analyse the components and understand the difficulties of your students.

2. *Demonstration*

A good demonstration is crucial for skill acquisition. Show the whole process first with as much flair as you can (and you may decide to use a filmed or videotaped version, so that you can guarantee the quality of the demonstration). This will help your students at the cognitive or plan formation stage (see Fitts & Posner, 1968; Welford, 1976). You will probably not attempt to talk your way through this part. Then break down what you have done into its component parts. Go through each of these stages (elements) again; keep it simple, giving the key points in advance. 'Talk through' your actions and any criterion checks or measurements that you make. Many teachers find that it takes some time for them to acquire fluent 'talk through' techniques. Don't be downhearted if it does not come easily to you. Avoid overloading students with too much information during your demonstration. It is better for them to concentrate on 'doing'. You can add information about standards and the background theory later.

Try to show the skill from the operator's point of view and position the students accordingly. Many tutors will be familiar with the overhead mirrors used in demonstration kitchens and some lecture theatres, which enable students to see what is happening. These are very useful, as is a video camera, but we cannot all be that fortunate in the type of equipment that may be available. Therefore, make sure that everyone can see what is going on. You may have to give certain demonstrations to small groups instead of to the whole class, so plan your overall lesson strategy accordingly so that those not watching can be meaningfully employed doing something else.

A good demonstration has vividness and clarity, and is an easily observed and understood sequence of steps and key points.

3. *Practice*

Let students practise the skill as soon as they can; supply plenty of prompts in writing (cards or handouts), large diagrams on the chalkboard/whiteboard, or even 'cues' in the form of finished products for students to handle, smell, taste and look at. Students should be given the opportunity to have their skill tested at once by performing under the direction of the teacher, and to be re-taught by the teacher if necessary.

Consider the use of video in your lessons, both for live or recorded demonstration and for the playback of students' own performance. Look for inventive ways to utilise such resources in your teaching. Many 'theory' classes would benefit from re-viewing a skill which had previously been demonstrated in the workshop and noting how the theoretical principles relate to what is actually done in practice.

Most important of all you need to provide feedback to students. Reinforce the good responses and indicate to them when and where they need to improve their performance. You will also need to be sensitive to the progress of your students and take action to help motivate them through any learning plateaus (see Annett, 1989).

Research indicates the optimum distribution of practice for acquiring skills. For example, it is claimed that badminton/squash performance improves most effectively with practice three times a week. Doing more or less than this realises only diminishing returns. You will need to do some research and find out what is the best distribution of practice for the skills you teach. Your own experience as a learner of those skills will provide guidance.

References

Annet J (1989) 'Skills' in AM Coleman & JG Beaumont (eds) *Psychology survey 7* British Psychological Society and Routledge

Fitts P & Posner M (1968) *Human performance* Prentice Hall

Hayes N (1998) *Foundations of psychology* Routledge

Welford AT (1976) *Skilled performance: perceptual & motor skills* Scott, Foresman

2. Cognitive Learning

Leslie B Curzon

1. The Cognitive School

Behaviourism ... has found the door, but it still lacks the key to what is beyond. 'We' do not just sit within the skin and observe. 'We' also infer and interpret what 'we' observe. And if 'we' are naught but representational processes, then 'we' know 'we' exist because those processes think.

(Wyers, 1988)

'Cognitive psychology is concerned with how organisms cognize – gain knowledge about – their world, and how they use that knowledge to guide decisions and perform effective actions' (Bower & Hilgard)[1].   The process of cognition is perceived as involving the overall functioning of a complex system of unobservable mental abilities (remembering, reasoning, etc.) which is the key to the manipulation of information. The tenets of the cognitive school are in total opposition to those of the behaviourists; it is the learner, not the learning task, which is of significance; the emphasis in any explanation of learning has to be placed on mental structure, strategy and organization, not on the S-R model, and internal processes and innate factors must be emphasized in discussions on learning. (The theory of 'innate categories of thought', suggesting that innate faculties such as causality and necessity give structure and meaning to our experience, was first enunciated by the philosopher Kant, 1724–1804).

Cognitivism makes wide use of analogies in order to explain the processes of cognition. A popular analogy is that of information processing and the input-output capacity of the computer. The learner is viewed as an information processor who discriminates among the input of stimuli to his or her sensory organs, detects regularities in accordance with his or her patterns of experience, and uses these regularities to solve problems in a manner which renders possible the coding of any further input.   The 'cognitive product' is the direct result of 'cognitive processes' transforming, reducing, elaborating and storing cognitive (i.e. sensory) input.[2]

Cognitive processing can be inferred as applying to all types of information. Hence students' learning can be analyzed in terms of a single unitary model. Further, in the teaching-learning context, the relation between cognitive processing and environmental events is reciprocal.   Students are, therefore, not merely passive recipients of information: they 'create' what teaching means to them, so that it is incorrect to view their achievements as resulting solely from the teacher's activities. The role of mental structure and its organization should be seen as vital in the learning process. By 'structure', cognitivists mean the properties of intellect that are inferred as governing behaviour. Learning is viewed as the modification of these structures.

9

Dick[3] emphasizes the significance for cognitive psychology in the area of instruction of 'schemata', that is the active organization by the learner of his or her past reactions and experiences. Instruction involves the storage of new information in previously created schemata, the recall of previously learned verbal information, the alteration of new information so that it fits in with existing schemata, the enabling of learners to make inferences so as to fill in any gaps in existing schemata, and the general modification of schemata.

The tenets of cognitive psychology have an immediate appeal for many teachers. The teaching environment does appear to convey information which students process. It seems as though students act so as to make sense out of their environment by selecting important stimuli; some aspects of the environment are rejected, some are utilized. Cognitive characteristics, such as prior levels of student attainment, general mental abilities, developed memory functions, do appear to account in large measure for achievement. If teachers wish to understand the processes which are presumed to take place privately within the student, the analogy of information processing does appear to offer some assistance.

Dewey, Bruner and Ausubel ... were involved in an analysis of the purposes of education and the practical problems of the classroom. Vygotsky devoted much of his short career to investigating the relation of thought to language – a fundamental aspect of the process of instruction. For him, and other cognitive psychologists, the task of the teacher is seen as related directly to the development of cognitive strategies within the student, so that he may improve his capabilities in selecting and modulating his internal processes of thinking, perceiving and learning.

Some of the objections to cognitive theory are mentioned below. Skinner, in particular, sought to rebut the arguments of the cognitivists. Thus, in *The Selection of Behaviour* (1989), he makes the following points (see also Skinner's 'Why I am not a cognitive psychologist'[4]):

> *I like Marr's statement that 'modern cognitive psychology largely views the behaviour of organs as symptomatic of internal information processing – activities comfortably expressed in computer metaphor'. The important word is 'comfortably'. The computer is a model of one kind of human behaviour, anticipated thousands of years ago with clay tiles in which information is 'stored and retrieved' for computational purposes. But it is not a useful model of the organism that engages in that behaviour, and the comfort will, I am sure, be short-lived.*
>
> *Cognitive psychology has tried to improve both observation and inference concerning the state of the body that is felt as belief, knowledge, intention, or expectation. I think it has faced insuperable difficulties, and in the long run it will have done nothing more than improve a vocabulary useful for non-scientific purposes...*

Notes and references: the Cognitive School

1. See generally: 'Recent developments in cognitive theories' by G Bower & E Hilgard; *Cognitive Psychology* by D Medin & B Ross (Harcourt Brace, 1996); *Cognitive Psychology*

(ed) C French (Longman, 1993); *Cognitive Psychology* by M Eysenck (Erlbaum, 1996); *Cognitive Psychology and Instruction* by R Brunning (Merrill, 1995); *Cognitive Psychology* by JB Best (West, 1995); *Dictionary of Cognitive Psychology* by I Stuart-Hamilton (Kingsley, 1991); *The Science of the Mind* (ed) RL Solso (OUP, 1995); *How Brains Think* by WH Calvin (Weidenfeld & Nicolson, 1997); *Cognition* by D Reisberg (Norton, 1997).

2. Not all psychologists accept the force of this analogy. Neisser points out that in a computer the hardware and software have no influence on each other, but in the human organism they do. 'The human is a special kind of biological processor and I suspect that surprising little of what we know of ... computers applies to the human': D Norman in 'A psychologist views human processing' in *Proceedings of the International Joint Commission on Artificial Intelligence* (1981).

3. With Gagné, 'Instructional Psychology' in *Annual Review of Psychology* (1983: 34).

4. *Behaviourism* (1977, 5); see also 'Cognitive Science and Behaviourism' by BF Skinner in *British Journal of Psychology* (1985: 76).

2. Theories of information processing and memory

Do not be impressed by all that is presumably known about the psychology of memory. Less is known than you might think... How do we remember stories, events, and experiences? More to the point, how do we retrieve them when least we expect them?

(Norman, 1980)

... The subject matter of this chapter is the range of processes known as *memory* (remembering and forgetting)...[1]

The cumulative effects of students' past learning experiences will exert their influence on their present behaviour. The capacity to understand the present so as to plan for the future demands from students some ability to draw on past experiences; they can bridge the present and the future by utilizing their memory of the past. Whether memory exists as an active process or a mere 'storage bin' remains a subject of research from which teachers may learn much. The controversy has stimulated investigation into what is inferred as happening when a student finds one topic 'easy to remember', but has much difficulty in recalling another. It has also provoked discussion and experiment into why retrieval failure is more marked in some circumstances than others.

Neisser[2] has suggested that too many laboratory experiments into memory are proving less productive than research based on 'naturalistic study': the place to investigate student learning is, he believes, in the classroom, not the laboratory. Attention has also been drawn to the 'fuzzy' nature of the phenomenon of remembering, often rendering precise investigation difficult.

Bartlett states:[3]

Remembering is not a re-excitation of innumerable fixed, lifeless and fragmentary traces. It is an imaginative reconstruction, or construction, built out of the relation of our attitude towards a whole active mass of organized

11

past reactions or experience, and to a little outstanding detail which commonly appears in image or in language form. It is thus hardly ever really exact, even in the most rudimentary cases of rote-recapitulation, and it is not at all important that it should be.

Analogies and the use of models ... are common in memory research. Memory has been considered in terms of clay tablets on which impressions and traces are made; it has been visualized as a telephone exchange and, more recently, in terms of information processing and the computer. Where analogies illustrate and lead to the construction of hypotheses, they are of value; where they provide the basis for models which rely on some few similarities while ignoring many others, they may have a restricted value. Teachers should keep in mind their own experiences concerning students who seem to remember easily, and those who quickly forget the simplest data. The theories presented below should be considered alongside those experiences.

Retention and recall of knowledge: the problem

'I revised the work with them only last week and today they can't answer a single question about it!' Statements of this nature must have been made in most college staffrooms at one time or another. They express the bewilderment of the teacher confronted by a class unable to recall the content of a recent lesson. For students, too, there is dismay in discovering that, although they can recall effortlessly the words and tune of a song heard (and never consciously 'learned') five years ago, they cannot recall lesson material 'committed to memory' five days ago. It is a responsibility of the teacher-manager to arrange instruction so that knowledge is retained by the learner.

Three important questions arise:

1. What is the basis of 'memory'?
2. Why do we forget?
3. How can the process of instruction be structured so as to aid retention and recall?

The memory

Memory, writes Doyle[4], refers to the ability to bring to mind past events whose characters, locations, happenings, or materials are no longer present to our senses. 'Memory is a bridge over the flow of time ... but many psychologists have concluded that it is both less and more than an inner record of all the events we live through.'

By 'memory' we refer to those processes essential for most intelligent behaviour, including learning, by which a person is able to recall past experiences to his present consciousness. Smith[5] speaks of it as 'an organized and integrative process combining both perceptual and motor activities'. Evans[6] defines it as 'essentially that property, shared by a large number of living organisms, of storing information about past experiences so that these can be acted on later to improve the animal's chances of surviving'. Gerard[7] states: 'Memory involves the making of an impression by an experience, the retention of some record of this impression and the re-entry of this record into consciousness (or behaviour) as recall and recognition'. Adams[8] views memory as 'the habit state of a subject that gives the capacity for correct recurrences of a criterion response'.

There can be no learning without remembering; but learning and remembering are not equivalents, they are different aspects of the same phenomenon. To remember is to retain the effects of experience over a time; to learn is to retain information over a period of time. Hence, memory is implicit in all types of learning. 'There could be no learning if there were no memory, for the effects of experience could not carry over from one time to the next' (Donahoe & Wessells).[9]

In order to demonstrate that a student has *learned*, it is necessary to show that he or she has *remembered*, i.e. that, given the passage of time and the effects of interference, the student is able, nevertheless, to retain and retrieve information learned on a previous occasion.

The comments above concerning the phenomenon we speak of as 'remembering' should serve to remind teachers that memory is probably not a 'central storehouse' located at some fixed points in the brain. Rather is it to be thought of as a series of functions of the central nervous system, involving the registration and storing of an individual's experiences and the later recall of what has been stored.

The views of early physiologists, such as Gall (1758–1828) and Flourens (1794–1867), suggesting that mental powers, such as memory, were localized in separate, identifiable regions of the brain, seem to have been discredited by the work of Lashley and Penfield. (Lashley has argued that functions are not localized, but that every region of the brain is involved in all functions – the notion of 'equipotentiality'.)

Luria, the Russian neuropsychologist, argues that no psychological ability exists in isolation and that human mental processes in general, and conscious activity in particular, require the participation of *all* the appropriate functional units of the brain. A commonly held view of many brain research workers is summarized by Stein & Rosen: 'In contrast to the view of functional localization, we are proposing that the brain be viewed as a dynamic organization of differentiated, but highly interrelated, structures... Input into any one area of the central nervous system can affect activity in all areas of the brain'.[10] Note, however, experiments in electrical stimulation of the brain by Ojemann in 1990 (mentioned by Crick[11]) involving a bilingual person, and suggesting a difference in the location of certain aspects of that person's two languages.

The information-processing model of the memory

In recent years several 'models of memory', i.e. representations of systems believed to account for the phenomena involved in remembering, have been constructed. A number of these models reflect the 'information-processing' approach, which views the memory system as involving three sequential processes – *registration, retention,* and *retrieval of information.* (It will be noted that the language used here is metaphorical, i.e. the processes are explained in terms associated with the storage and retrieval of information in a computer.)

a) *Registration* comprises the perception, encoding, and neural representation of stimuli at the time of a learning experience. Perception involves the set of events following stimulation that occur in the brain's input part. Encoding involves the selectivity of registration: perceived stimuli are transformed into an organized, conceptual 'meaningful' mode. Encoding processes may emerge as diagrams, images, etc. The teacher should note that a student's motivation, attention, previously acquired knowledge, will affect the selection of stimuli for registration.

b) *Retention* allows the neurological representation of the student's experiences to be 'stored' over a period of time for later use. (Hence, to 'forget' may be considered as failure to retain that which has been registered.) Tulving[12] has suggested that 'learning' is merely an improvement in the student's power of retention.

c) *Retrieval* allows the student to have access to information previously registered and retained. It may be that the mechanism of retrieval is distinct from that which places information in the memory. Eccles[13] suggests that 'databank memory' is stored in the brain, especially in the cerebral cortex, and is retrieved by a mental act. 'Recognition memory' then allows critical scrutiny of the retrieval; that scrutiny continues until the retrieval is judged to be correct, or is abandoned. Note Bartlett's suggestion that the act of remembering is more like 'reconstructing' than 'locating or fishing out'.

The Waugh-Norman model[14] suggests that items first enter one's primary memory (PM), which has a very limited capacity. Rehearsal (i.e. 'going over' something in one's memory repeatedly) maintains the items in the PM and assists in transferring them to the more permanent secondary memory (SM). When new material is introduced to the PM, old material is displaced. An item in the PM is in the student's consciousness; an item recalled from the SM has been absent from his or her consciousness.

The Atkinson-Shiffrin model[15] involves three components: a sensory memory, a short-term store (STS), and a long-term store (LTS). The information in one's sensory memory (resulting from simple sensory recognition of stimuli), also known as 'surface memory', lasts only a fraction of a second, depending on the strength of the stimuli (an important point for teachers); such information is made up, according to Houston, of 'very basic, unelaborated impressions of the external environment which decay rapidly unless processed into one of the other stores'. (An example might be a word spoken by the teacher which results in the learner having to integrate his or her changing pattern of auditory stimulation.)

Some of the information in the sensory memory is transferred, as the result of maintaining the process of attention, to the STS. (Cognitive psychologists say that the STS defines our immediate consciousness.) Information may be lost from the STS in about 15–20 seconds by a process of displacement or lack of rehearsal; it is transferred to the LTS as the result of processing, i.e. rehearsal. ('Maintenance rehearsal', known also as 'rote rehearsal' or 'repetition', is intended to hold information for immediate use. 'Elaborative rehearsal' attempts to relate newly acquired information to patterns of knowledge stored in LTS.)

14

Information in the LTS may remain there permanently, although it is subject to interference and a process of decay. It is the LTS which is of much interest to the teacher; it represents the permanent part of the learner's memory system reserved for information of high future utility (e.g. one's native language).

A much-simplified diagram, illustrating the basic features of this model is given in Figure 1.

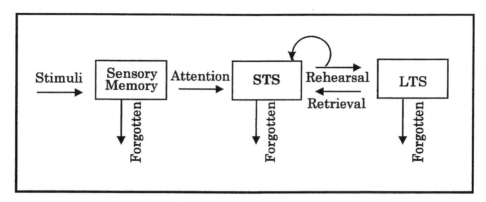

Figure 1   The Atkinson-Shiffrin model of memory

Theoreticians, such as Tulving,[16] have suggested that the long-term memory can be divided into *episodic memory* which stores images of our personal experiences, *semantic memory* which stores facts and general knowledge, and *procedural memory* which stores information about how to perform activities. Johnson[17] states that the long-term memory (LTM) is of particular importance in learning: 'Learning may be said to be *meaningful* to the extent that the new learning task can be related [in the LTM] to the existing cognitive structure of the learner, i.e. the residual of his earlier learnings.' The degree of 'meaningfulness' will depend on the learner's associational background, recorded in his or her LTM.

Cognitive psychologists, such as Anderson,[18] have argued that information in the LTM is organized as *schemata*, that is abstract structures of information. The schemata provide expectations about objects and events; when they are properly formed and a particular event is consistent with our expectations, comprehension emerges. Anderson suggests, further, that it is when students do not possess appropriate schemata that problems of memory, comprehension and behaviour may emerge.

Broadbent's model[19] comprises three stores – sensory memory, STS and LTS – and, between STS and LTS, there is an 'address register' which holds information about items that assist in the retrieval of matter from LTS by 'reminding' the individual of what action is to be undertaken in the process of search.

The Craik-Lockhart[20] 'levels of processing' theory states that learners appear to subject stimuli to varying levels of mental processing. Learners retain only that information which has been thoroughly processed so that 'meaning' is given to it. The more attention given to the details of a stimulus, the more likely the student is to remember those details. Bransford[21] has suggested an amendment to this theory by advocating the significance for memory of the *depth of processing* and the *similarities* between the conditions under which the material was learned and those under which its reinstatement is required.

The concept of memory as involving the processing of information in the form of a progression through distinct memory stores has been criticized for failing to stress the *dynamic nature* of memory. It is suggested, as an alternative, that *levels of processing* be emphasized, so that there need be no clear 'terminal points' separating one store from another; memory codes should be characterized according to the degree of processing that created them. Thus, the durability of the memory trace will increase as the depth of processing increases. To retrieve deeply-processed information may require more processing capacity than that needed to retrieve shallow-processed information...

Why we forget

Inability to recall (i.e. the process whereby information in the memory becomes inaccessible) or recognize may range in intensity from the momentary 'slip of memory' (so that one refers to one's friend, George, as John, and quickly corrects the error) to the functional disturbances of the memory such as amnesia, as a result of which the sufferer cannot recall immediate personal history.

A variety of reasons for the phenomenon of forgetting can be advanced: repression (i.e. motivated forgetting – a defence mechanism which seems to allow us to set aside and render inaccessible very unpleasant memories); disuse of information (leading, presumably, to the disappearance of the associated memory traces); trace decay; cue-forgetting; and interference.

Trace decay (i.e. gradual decay or loss of clarity in the neural engram) is inferred from the phenomenon which is illustrated in Figure 2, i.e. the well-known 'curve of forgetting', representing a decline in the amount remembered over a period of time (if the material learned is not 'practised').

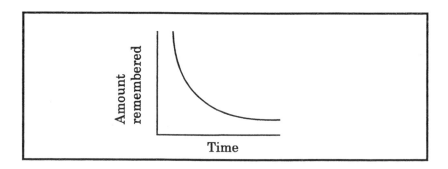

Figure 2 Curve of forgetting

16

(It should be noted that the amount which the learner tends to forget does *not* vary in direct proportion to the passing of time – there is a gradual levelling out of the curve after an initial steep decline.) It has been suggested that traces in the learner's perceptual system tend to fade rapidly immediately after presentation. Thus, according to Thorndike, if actions fall into disuse and are not practised, they weaken and disappear from the memory. (Teachers are often intuitively aware of this.) Guthrie argued that forgetting occurs as the result of competition among responses. Many psychologists now believe that the passing of time does not in itself explain forgetting; the passing of time permits interference from new learning and other memories, which produces forgetting. The nature of the learner's activities between learning and attempted recall is also significant in strengthening or diminishing the capacity to remember. The relevance of this to the place of emphasis, recapitulation and revision in the planning of a lesson should be clear.

Cue-dependent forgetting refers to a failure of retrieval because the cues which were present at the time of learning are not present at the moment of attempted recall. There is a 'trace', but the lack of appropriate cues prevents the learner's access to that trace. Provision by the teacher of contextual cues is useful: 'While you are trying to recall this, think of last week's lesson in which we looked at a video. Can you recall the first event which was shown?'

Interference refers to the inhibition of one 'piece of learning' by another. Where the learner forgets something because of something else he learns *afterwards*, the effect is known as *retroactive inhibition*. Where he forgets something because of something else he has learned before, the effect is known as *proactive inhibition*. Experimental groups have been used to study interference in the following ways:

Experimental group	Learn A	Learn B	Recall A
Control group	Learn A	Rest	Recall A

(Here the measure of *retroactive inhibition* is the difference in recall.)

Experimental group	Learn B	Learn A	Recall A
Control group	Rest	Learn A	Recall A

(Here the measure of *proactive inhibition* is the difference in recall.)

The more similar the subject matter learned (as tasks A and B), the greater is the possibility of interference, resulting in forgetting. The importance of this finding for the management of the teaching process needs to be stressed: timetables should be arranged so as to separate as widely as is practicable subjects with a similar content, e.g. foreign languages.

Further, since interference seems very powerful over short periods of time, the importance in verbal communication of leaving a short gap after a significant statement is based not on any practice of the art of rhetoric but on the need to allow time for some fact to 'sink in' so that its chances of being retained by the learner are increased.[33]

17

(Teachers who are planning lesson content should be aware of the 'primary' and 'recency' effects, which are said to explain the general tendency of students to learn best the first and last things presented in a lesson: the introductory and concluding parts of a unit of instruction are of special significance for the remembering of information. As a consequence, the 'middle of the lesson' should be carefully reinforced. Note also the so-called 'serial position effect' from which is derived the advice: 'Put forward the most important material at the beginning and end of the lesson; do not bury it in the middle'.)

Osgood comments:

> *A memory is nothing more than a response produced by a stimulus. It is merely the maintained association of a response with a stimulus over an interval of time. The question of why we forget comes down to this: what are the conditions under which stimuli lose their capacity to evoke previously associated responses? Forgetting is a direct function of the degree to which substitute responses are associated with the original stimuli during the retention interval.* [34]

There is also evidence that trying to learn too much may result in forgetting, since the short-term memory may have a capacity of not more than 7±2 separate 'chunks'. (Miller[35] has argued that the short-term memory is limited by its ability to handle only a limited number of chunks of information. In Miller's terminology, a 'chunk' is a unit which integrates a number of smaller elements into a meaningful whole. The size of a chunk can be enlarged by its integration within a hierarchy, allowing the learner's capacity to pay attention to new information to be increased by stages.) This, too, has significance for the planning of instruction, in particular for the timing and spacing of lesson content.

Failure of recall may be the result of the teacher's understandable wish to impart as much information as time will allow, without taking into account the possible over-burdening of the students' short-term memory. 'Mental indigestion' may be an imprecise metaphor; it draws attention, however, to the difficulties for the student who is required to assimilate a large mass of material in a short period.

Koestler's 'abstractive' and 'spotlight' memories

In an interesting paper, supported by some experimental detail, Koestler[36] advanced a hypothesis involving two types, or categories, of memory – abstractive and spotlight. Both are different classes of phenomena, based on different neural mechanisms. Abstractive memory generalizes and schematizes; spotlight memory particularizes and concretizes.

Abstractive memory which, in the learner, is related to insightful learning, comprises what we can remember of our life history and the knowledge we have accumulated. A process of filtering 'strips down' input to bare essentials; we condense, remember sequences and reduce experience to a colourless abstract before it moves into the memory store. ('A large proportion of our memories resembles the dregs in a wine glass, the dehydrated sediments of experiences whose flavour has gone.') Learners retain the abstracted meaning of the instruction they have received; particulars may be lost, but they can be trained by appropriate teaching (and by learning from experience) to abstract fine nuances, enabling them to recall detail.

Spotlight memory is derived from our ability to recall episodes from the past with almost hallucinatory vividness. This adds texture and flavour to what is recalled because it is powerfully evocative. Some emotional significance may be involved in retention of this nature; it is as if a significant experience has been imprinted in the memory. The past is continuously recreated in the forms of eidetic imagery (i.e. of a richly pictorial quality). The amalgam of spotlight and abstractive memory affects the content and flavour of our total recall, and the processes involved (which are not yet understood and can only be inferred) are largely of an unconscious nature. 'The canons of perception and memory operate instantaneously and unconsciously; we are always playing games without awareness of the rules.'

The teacher's role in aiding retention and recall

The practical experience of teachers, underpinned by some of the theory discussed earlier in this chapter, may indicate that the learner can be aided in tasks of memorization, consolidation and recall if lesson preparation takes into account certain matters. These are considered under six headings: timetabling, content, preparedness, presentation, revision, and practice...

Timetabling

The timetabling of a course ought to take into consideration the difficulties which might arise for the learner as the result of proactive and retroactive inhibition. Timetabling should 'space out' similar subjects, should allow for breaks, and should not overload the student with long, unvaried lesson periods so charged with material that acquisition and retention become impossible. (Teachers should note and consider the implications of the discovery by the Gestalt psychologist, Zeigarnik, that interrupting a task in which a learner has become involved, can lead to a higher level of recall of the material being learned. The memory traces which are said to be associated with incomplete actions are thought to remain active until completion of the task.)

Content

The content of the lesson ought to be presented not as an isolated unit but, essentially, as a continuation of that which has been learned previously. It ought to be associated clearly with the learner's existing stock of knowledge. 'The more other facts a fact is associated with in the mind the better possession of it our memory retains. Each of its associates becomes a hook to which it hangs, a means to fish it up by when sunk beneath the surface' (James). (James believed that the secret of a good memory was the forming of 'diverse and multiple associations with every fact we care to retain... All improvement in memory consists in the improvement of one's habitual methods of recording facts.') As noted above, the provision of cues for the recall of relevant information is also an important contribution the teacher can make to the process of assisting retention and recall. Perhaps above all, the content of the lesson must be *meaningful* to the learner if it is to lead to firm retention and swift recall.

19

Meaningful material is usually remembered more clearly and for longer periods of time than that which has little or no relation to the student's level of learning at the time of the lesson. The statement couched in simple terms, introducing new concepts in terms of those which are already known, has a higher chance of acquisition than that which goes outside the student's conceptual framework, thus making comprehension and retention very difficult. 'If the material is sufficiently meaningful, there may be no forgetting whatever. Content that is not so brilliantly structured, but that still has much meaning, will be remembered in proportion to its meaning. Nonsense material is headed for extinction before the last syllable is uttered' (Stephens & Evans).[37]

Preparedness
Preparedness involves the teacher's explanation, in carefully contrived terms, of the significance and usefulness of the learning in relation to the learner's life style. Seligman has suggested that memory may be related directly to the learner's preparedness. It is for the teacher to motivate the learner in a manner which will arouse and maintain personal involvement with the topic which is to be remembered.

Presentation
Presentation of the lesson, if it is to aid retention, demands a logical, clearly connected and organized sequence. The short-term memory seems to be associated with the organization of information; hence adequate rehearsal is important if information is to be retained more or less permanently. Where the parts of the lesson are organized coherently, comprehension, acquisition and retention of the whole ought to be facilitated since patterns are usually more acceptable to the learner than disjointed fragments. (William James[38] pointed out that, 'of two men with the same outward experiences and the same amount of mere native tenacity, the one who thinks over his experiences most and weaves them into systematic relations with each other will be the one with the best memory'.) A 'warm-up period', particularly before relearning, is usually beneficial to the student's recall processes. Further, the student should be stimulated by the presentation so that his attention (i.e. surface memory) remains focused on the lesson material, thus assisting assimilation and retention. Wherever possible, the presentation ought to avoid an outcome which is no more than rote-learning. (Ausubel describes rote-learned materials as 'discrete and relatively isolated entities that are relatable to cognitive structure only in an arbitrary, verbatim fashion'.) The presenter should aim, rather, at the achievement of insight and the understanding of principles which will facilitate retention. Principles are generally retained much more effectively than a mass of material which has been committed to memory without understanding. Note, also, the *von Restorff effect*, which suggests that the teacher can assist memorization by making ideas stand out, e.g. by verbal exaggeration, underlining, use of bold print and colour in writing.

In *Memory and Program Construction* (1979),[39] Ludwig, who had investigated the problems of retention by students of the content of instruction, argues that where a teacher attempts to make a number of points during a half-hour lesson period, no more than twenty of those points will find a place in a student's short-term memory. Of those twenty points, only six or seven will move into the long-term memory. But the number of points which move into the long-term memory may be doubled where the content of the lesson is repeated some two or three weeks later.

Presentation of the lesson might include training in the use of peg words, key words and mnemonics. Advice from the teacher on the use of a peg words, which, when recalled in the appropriate context, will assist in the recall of associated words, can be valuable. A lecturer dealing with the concept of entropy in a unit of instruction as part of a course in introductory thermodynamics can use as peg words, 'distribution of energy', 'measure of information'. Key words, when supplied by the teacher, can lead to the recall of structures and schemas of thought. An economics teacher conducting a course on 'protection' might use as key words 'dumping', 'diversification', etc. Mnemonics (Greek, *mnasthai* = to remember) can be presented by the teacher as aids to the memorizing of sequences: they are coined words and phrases that use the initials of the words to be remembered in their correct order. Examples: '(Mr.) Roy G. Biv' (red, orange, yellow ... etc. – the order of colours of the spectrum); 'FACE', to indicate the notes in the spaces of the five-line musical stave; the ludicrous, but useful, statement intended to assist students of anatomy in remembering the order of the twelve cranial nerves: 'At an oil factory (*olfactory*), an optician (*optic*) searched for the occupant (*oculomotor*) of a truck (*trochlear*) which...'[40]

Revision and practice

Assimilation, consolidation and retention of lesson content require recapitulation, rehearsal, *periodic revision and review* (i.e. 'practice with an experimental cast'). The teacher's recapitulation at regular intervals of the lesson headings may help in their assimilation. Rehearsal – by which is meant an activity in which the student goes over the lesson material *by himself* after its initial presentation (which may be equivalent to a repetition of the lesson's stimuli) – can take the form of reading a handout which contains a summary of the lesson's main points, or studying and reciting one's own notes. (Such an activity is an example of the 'deep processing' which is said to improve the memory, in that it contributes to the durable encoding of lesson content in the long-term memory.) Revision – which involves re-studying the lesson – should take place as soon as possible after the lesson has ended. (Note the work of Garcia, which throws doubt on the tenet that learning can take place *only* when stimulus and associable events are close in time.) It should be repeated at intervals and, preferably, be linked with tests which examine recall. (There is evidence to suggest that the 'distribution of practice' does affect speed of learning *and* efficiency of recall. The spacing of recall tests is, therefore, of much importance in lesson planning.) The final revision ought to be planned by the class teacher and could be the occasion for a full examination which will test and assess the level of comprehension and recall. Davies suggests that recall tends to rise to its maximum point about ten minutes after the conclusion of a lesson, and that this may be the result of the mind's 'putting material into focus'. A very steep decline in remembering then takes place and, by the next day, approximately 75 per cent of the lesson may have failed to move into the long-term memory. Frequent and spaced reviews of lesson content are essential if learning is to be effective.

The assimilation of material presented in class, the building and maintenance of memory, may be assisted by the process of its being applied in *practice situations*. In particular, where psychomotor skills are being taught, practice ought to walk hand in hand with theory rather than follow on its heels. Thus, the theory of the use of the navigational compass is best assimilated by the learner who is able to participate in planned projects involving the practical use of the instrument.

The concept of *circadian rhythms* might be considered by the teacher planning a programme of instruction. It is suggested that there is a daily pattern of physiological change in our bodies which affects our information-processing capacities. Short-term retention, it is argued, is better in the morning; long-term retention seems to be better when the student is learning material in the afternoon. Wingfield argues that biological rhythms have a large effect on performance and memory – up to 10–20 per cent of a total performance score.

Strategies for memorisation

In relation to the tasks of verbal learning, Slavin[41] enumerates the following positive methods: use of mental imagery (involving the visualization of 'vivid key words'); use of mnemonics; massed practice (i.e. learning facts by repeating them on many random occasions during a time period); distributed practice (repeating items at fixed intervals during a time period); part learning (learning and seeking to memorize the material, one segment at a time); overlearning (involving practising newly acquired knowledge after the achievement of mastery).

Fontana[42] advises the following routines so as to assist consolidation and improvement of the efficiency of the long-term memory: repeating material and questioning the learner; making instruction relevant, understandable and interesting; introducing practice into the learning process; practising recognition and recall. Davies recommends employment of the following instructional tactics: concentration on the sequencing of instruction; attempting to stress key points by emphasizing essential facts; organization of teaching material into patterns by the use of diagrams and charts; stressing relationships of newly learned material and that which is already known...

Notes and references: information-processing and memory

1. See generally: *Human Memory* by A Baddeley (Erlbaum, 1994); *Theories of Memory* (ed) A F Collins (Erlbaum, 1996); *Memory in the Real World* by G Cohen (Erlbaum, 1996); *Memory* (ed) E L Bjork (Academic Press, 1996); *The Anatomy of Memory* (ed) J McConkey (OUP, 1996); *Memory* by A Parkin (Blackwell, 1996).
2. *Memory Observed* (Freeman, 1982).
3. *Remembering* (CUP, 1932).
4. *Explorations in Psychology* by C L Doyle (Brooks, 1987).
5. *Cybernetic Principles of Learning and Educational Design* (Holt, Rinehart & Winston, 1966).
6. *Psychology: A Dictionary of the Mind, Brain and Behaviour* (Arrow Books, 1978).
7. 'The memory' in *Scientific American* (1953, 2).
8. *Human Memory* (McGraw-Hill, 1969).
9. *Learning, Language and Memory* (Harper & Row, 1980).
10. Note, however, the work of researchers such as Zeki, of London University. He apparently identified the existence and location of a specialised 'colour centre' in the

brain: *Nature* (1989, p.386). See also *A Vision of the Brain* by S. Zeki (Blackwell, 1993); *The Human Brain* by S. Greenfield (Weidenfeld & Nicolson, 1997).

11. *The Astonishing Hypothesis* (Simon & Schuster, 1994).
12. *Elements of Episodic Memory* (OUP, 1983).
13. *The Self and Its Brain* by Sir Karl Popper and Sir John Eccles (Routledge & Kegan Paul, 1984). This notable review of the body-mind relationship contains much information of interest to the teacher who wishes to know 'how we function'. It includes, for example, an explanation of current theories concerning the function of the brain hemispheres. (Note an argument against the 'right brain, left brain' hypothesis in 'Right brain, left brain: fact and fiction' by J. Levy in *Contemporary Issues in Educational Psychology* (McGraw-Hill, 1987).
14. 'Primary memory' in *Psychological Review* (1965, 72).
15. 'Human memory' in the *Psychology of Learning and Motivation* (Academic Press, 1968).
16. 'How many memory systems are there?' in *American Psychologist*, (1985, 40).
17. 'Meaning in complex learning' in *Review of Educational Research* (1995).
18. 'Some reflections on the acquisition of knowledge' in *Educational Research* (1984, 13).
19. *Perception and Communication* (Pergamon, 1958).
20. 'A framework for memory research' in *Journal of Verbal Thinking* (1972, 11).
21. *Learning, Understanding and Remembering* (Belmont, 1979)...

33. See 'Limits of memory' in *Mind in Science* by R L Gregory (Peregrine, 1984).
34. 'Method and theory' in *Experimental Psychology* (OUP, 1953).
35. 'The magical number 7±' in *Psychological Review* (1956, 63). See also *The Mystery of Number* by A Schimmell (OUP, 1993).
36. *Bricks to Babel* (Picador, 1980).
37. *Development and Classroom Learning* (Holt, Rinehart & Winston, 1973).
38. *Principles of Psychology* (Holt, 1890).
39. Pub. Buffalo (1979).
40. 'Mnemonic devices: classification, characteristics and criteria' by F S Bellezza in *Review of Educational Research* (1981, 51). See also 'Mnemonic methods to enhance storage and retrieval' in *Memory* (ed) E L Bjork (Academic Press, 1996).
41. *Education Psychology* (Prentice-Hall, 1988).
42. *Psychology for Teachers* (Macmillan, 1995).

3. Two cognitive learning theorists

David Ausubel

Ausubel (b. 1918) has carried out much of his work in the City University of New York in which he directed the Office of Research and Evaluation. The principles of his thought are set out in *Educational Psychology – A Cognitive View* (1968); his other important writings include *Theory and Problems of Adolescent Development* (1964) and *The Psychology of Meaningful Verbal Learning* (1963).

Educational psychology is, according to Ausubel, concerned primarily with 'the nature, conditions, outcomes, and evaluation of classroom learning'; it should not involve itself with topics such as the nature and development of needs, animal learning and conditioning. Further, it should take into account only those kinds of learning that take place in the classroom – reception and discovery learning (i.e. meaningful 'symbolic' learning). Rote learning and motor learning are considered by Ausubel to be so inconsequential a part of classroom learning as not to warrant consideration in a treatment of educational psychology. Ausubel's condemnation of much rote learning derives from his observation that it is based on isolated units of information that the learner is unable to relate to, or anchor within, his existing cognitive structures. (O'Neil[1] emphasizes this view: 'Rote memorization usually involves multiple readings of the material with little or no effort devoted to assimilation. Therefore, the material learned through this method usually is not meaningfully related to other stored information, which limits the facility with which such information can be retrieved at a later date'.)

Ausubel and the learning process

Ausubel postulates learners' cognitive structures as 'hierarchically organised in terms of highly inclusive concepts under which are subsumed less inclusive subconcepts and informational data'.

The principal factors influencing meaningful learning and retention are, according to Ausubel, the *substantive content* of a learner's structure of knowledge and the *organization* of that structure at any given time. If cognitive structure is unstable and disorganized it will inhibit meaningful learning; if it is stable and well-organized it will assist in such learning. To have appropriate background knowledge of concepts and principles is essential for problem-solving. Prior experience with related problems is necessary for a learner to deal successfully with novel situations.

Ausubel differentiates carefully 'reception' and 'discovery' learning. In *reception learning* a learner is presented with the *entire content* of what is to be learned in its *final form*; the presentation is meaningful if it allows him to integrate new ideas with existing knowledge schemes and reproduce it, with understanding, at some future date; but it will not be meaningful if it does not assist in the creation of new understanding. The presentation of a geometrical theorem in terms which give the learner an opportunity to comprehend its structure, is an example. *Discovery learning* involves the learner discovering independently the principal content of what has to be learned *before* it can be incorporated meaningfully into already existing cognitive structures.

Ausubel suggests that a condition for optimal learning is the placing of newly learned facts within a context for meaning. Following such learning, the student's capacity to transform facts and integrate them into previously acquired experience will be increased.

Discovery learning in Bruner's sense is criticized by Ausubel. He will not accept that *all* discovery learning is meaningful; indeed, he believes that students who have reached the early stages of cognitive development learn more effectively by reception techniques. Problem-solving ability, he argues, is not necessarily transferred to situations outside the context in which it was acquired. Further, the discovery approach is not always linked to intrinsic motivation. He poses a rhetorical question to those who urge the use of discovery learning in all learning situations: 'Is it intended that a student shall rediscover *every* principle set out in the subject syllabus?'

In rejecting some of Bruner's claims concerning the discovery method, Ausubel emphasizes meaning as involving 'cognitive equivalence'; there can be no meaning for the learner without the existence of a related cognitive structure. In learning, the student 'subsumes' material to his cognitive structure. As a result of methodical expository teaching, students are able to proceed directly to a level of abstract understanding that is 'qualitatively superior to the intuitive level in terms of generality, clarity, precision and explication'. (Ausubel uses 'subsume' in the sense of incorporating material into a structure which has been created by prior learning.) 'In any case, discovery techniques hardly constitute an effective primary means of transmitting the contents of an academic discipline.'

'Meaningful learning' – to which classroom activity should be directed – involves *the acquisition of new meanings*. New meanings allow a learner to relate and anchor new material to the relevant and inclusive concepts in his or her existing cognitive structure, to integrate the essence of new experiences with existing patterns; this is essentially an 'active' process. In contrast, rote learning does not result in the acquisition of new meanings; it involves no logical perception, no comprehension of relationships, but only arbitrary constructs. The basic type of meaningful learning is representational, that is, learning the meaning of symbols. 'Propositional learning' allows the learning of the meaning of verbal propositions expressing ideas other than those of representational equivalence. 'Concept learning' involves the acquisition of generic ideas. Each of these three types is important for true learning.

Ausubel has formulated the prerequisites for meaningful learning under two headings: first, that the learner must be disposed to relate new information to a prior structure in preference to engaging in rote learning (i.e. he must have the correct 'set' to the task); and, second, that the new information presented to the learner must be relatable to his prior knowledge on a non-arbitrary basis, that is the new information and that which is constituted in the learner's prior knowledge must be related conceptually ('the perception of a stimulus will be a function of the learner's background').

Sequential organization of learning is of considerable importance. The arrangement of topics in a subject matter field should be the result of an understanding by the teacher of the importance of the fundamental 'anchoring concepts'. A learning unit ought to be a link in a chain; its acquisition by the learner should be an achievement in its own right and should provide the appropriate scaffolding for the next unit in the sequence. Antecedent steps should be consolidated if the learning of subsequent steps is not to be vitiated. Consolidation requires, according to Ausubel, 'confirmation, correction, clarification, differential practice and review'.

Ausubel criticizes the Gestaltist concept of insight. He stresses the emergence of insight as dependent on the learner's prior experience. It rarely appears in the 'Eureka' form; it tends rather to follow 'a period of fumbling and search, of gradual emergence of a correct hypothesis'. It is important for the teacher to understand, however, the circumstances in which an apparently unproductive period of thought is followed by a sudden 'seeing the light'.

Ausubel's 'advance organizers': theory into practice

Ausubel has advocated the utilization of 'advance organizers' in the process of instruction.[2] Hilgard suggests that the fundamental idea of the organizer rests on early Gestaltist concepts of a sequence of information as being best learned by comprehending how it is organized and how its parts fit together. The advance organizer is a relatively short arrangement of introductory material, presented to the learner *before* the lesson, designed to cue his relevant prior knowledge, and presented at *a higher level of abstraction, generality and inclusiveness* than that of the planned lesson. It may take the form of a short statement in continuous prose, or prose interlaced with diagrams, or networks indicating relationships.

Ausubel states that the principal function of the organizer is 'to bridge the gap between what the learner knows and what he needs to know before he can successfully learn the task at hand'. Davies[3] sees the functions of the organizer as: the provision of a linking structure; the differentiation of ideas leading to their acquisition with clarity; and the preservation of the identity of new ideas, ensuring that they are not absorbed totally into an existing structure with the loss of their distinctive features. Gagné considers the principal function of the organizer to be the activation of pre-existing cognitive structures in the learner's memory, involving recall.

Examples of the use of organizers in courses offered by one college of further education have included: the issuing of a document on 'The psychological causes of conflict' prior to a unit of instruction on 'problems of change' (in a course for supervisory managers); the distribution of an essay on 'Renewal and survival' before a lesson on 'population density' (in a course planned for A level geography); the circulation of an article from a trade periodical concerning the long-term future of computer-generated art, prior to a series of lectures on the topic (as part of a course leading to the BTEC HNC in Design, Packaging and Display). Ausubel gives an example of learners' knowledge of the fundamental principles of Christianity utilised as an organizer in a course leading to an understanding of the principles of Buddhism.

'Expository organizers' are used whenever the new material is totally unfamiliar; they emphasize context and link the essence of the new material with some relevant previously acquired concepts. They are intended to remind the learner 'of meaningful context already available in the memory and relevant to the new learning'. 'Comparative organizers' are used when the material to be learned is not entirely novel. They are intended to point out ways in which that material resembles, and differs from, that which is already known.

Mayer[4] has constructed a checklist of questions to be asked and answered by the producer of advance organizers:

1. Does the organizer I have produced allow me to generate all, or some, of the logical relationships in the material to be learned?

2. Does it provide the learner with a method of relating unfamiliar to familiar material?

3. Does it allow the learner to use the content?

4. Is it likely that the student will normally fail to use his organizational capabilities in the case of material to be learned in the forthcoming lesson?

Problems related to the production and use of organizers have been noted by teachers in the further education sector. First, the considerable range of individual differences among learners in a class makes the production of a useful general organizer difficult. Secondly, there are problems in constructing the necessary learning structures in some subject areas: thus the highly structured sciences of physics and biology provide a contrast to the very debatable structures of some of the social sciences. Thirdly, the techniques necessary for designing satisfactory organizers can be time-consuming: Joyce & Weil[5] indicate that teachers intending to produce advance organizers require 'a strong grasp of their subject matter, including an understanding of its propositional structure' – in short, the contriving of an organizer can be a complex, laborious task.

Research into the use of organizers[6] suggests that they might be of considerable value where the learner may not be able to recognize prior knowledge as relevant and where the teacher wishes to focus students' attention on relationships among the linked parts of an idea and on connections between parts and the whole. Ausubel's own research suggests that the use of organizers can enhance the relationship between cognitive structure and new material, thus facilitating teaching and learning.

Ausubel's work and the teacher

Ausubel's emphasis on 'meaningful learning' will remind teachers that learning, designed to ensure mastery of a situation by an extension of the student's powers of reasoning, involves the careful *design of instruction* with that end in mind. His stress on linking units of instruction to form a continuous process necessitates a 'programmed' approach to classwork so that sequential learning might be achieved and the learner assisted in the discrimination of old and new ideas.

The principal function of the teacher is seen by Ausubel as 'the art and science of presenting ideas and information meaningfully and effectively' so that clear, stable and unambiguous meanings emerge in the process of instruction and are retained by the learner over a long period of time as an *organized body of knowledge*.

Ausubel suggests that class learning can be improved through use of the technique of 'progressive differentiation'. The most general, inclusive concepts of a subject discipline should be taught first, followed by the less inclusive concepts, thus setting the stage for the teaching of specific information. Ease of assimilation and retention of information should result, since the learner's cognitive structure will then contain stable 'hooks' on which new material can be placed. The learner must be helped to discriminate between old and new ideas; this may require the paraphrasing of new ideas. Concepts must not be taught in isolation; the teacher must provide a *framework* (related to the learner's existing knowledge) into which new concepts will fit with relative ease. Organizers will assist in relating new concepts to existing pivotal ideas. Ausubel advocates, additionally, the adoption of 'integrative reconciliation' in the classroom. This technique concerns the overall organization of content within a subject area. New ideas must be integrated with those previously learned during a course: it is unhelpful to students to devote one lesson, early in the course, to a discussion of ideas and concepts and to fail to refer to those concepts at later stages of the course. This is to introduce barriers between subject elements and relationships. There should be reference throughout the course to previously learned ideas, definitions and principles, so that they are integrated into course content as a whole.

The provision of information feedback (essentially a task for the teacher) is seen by Ausubel in terms of positive, cognitive effects on learning. Feedback can confirm appropriate meanings, correct mistakes and misconceptions and indicate how well the learning task has been mastered. 'As a result ... the subject's confidence in his learning product is increased, his learning is consolidated, and he is better able to focus his efforts and attention on those aspects of a task requiring further refinement.'[7]

On the matter of teacher responsibility for the content of the curriculum, Ausubel takes an uncompromising stand against the advocates of a system in which student decisions are used to determine that content. 'Teachers cannot in good conscience abdicate this responsibility [of structuring subject matter content] by turning over to students, in the name of democracy and progressivism, the direction of education.' The content of the curriculum takes into account the students' needs; its formulation remains, however, the teacher's, not the students' responsibility...

Notes and references: Ausubel

1. *Learning Strategies* (Academic Press, 1978).
2. See 'The use of advance organizers' in *Journal of Educational Psychology* (1960, 51); 'In defence of advance organizers' in *Review of Educational Research* (1978, 45); *Psychology Applied to Teaching* by R Biehler (Houghton-Mifflin, 1993).
3. *Objectives in Curriculum Design* (McGraw-Hill, 1976).
4. 'Can advance organizers influence meaningful learning?' in *Review of Educational Research* (1979, 49).
5. *Models of Teaching* (Prentice-Hall, 1980).
6. See e.g. 'Do advance organizers facilitate learning?' by B Barnes and ED Clawson in *Review of Educational Research* (1978, 45); 'Advance organizers as a teaching strategy' by J Lawton and S Wanska in *Review of Educational Research* (1977, 47).
7. *School Learning – An Introduction to Educational Psychology* (Holt, Rinehart & Winston, 1969)...

Jerome Bruner

> *Man is not a naked ape but a culture-clothed human being, hopelessly ineffective without the prosthesis provided by culture. The very nature of his characteristics as a species provides a guide to appropriate pedagogy, and the very nature of his nervous system and its constraints provides a basis for devising reasonable if not inevitable principles for designing a testable pedagogy.*

(Bruner, 1973)

This chapter considers the cognitive educational psychology associated with Bruner (b. 1916)[1], who draws upon a variety of disciplines such as biology, mathematics and social anthropology in order to fashion a doctrine of learning and a theory of instruction intended to assist in the creation of 'a better or happier or more courageous or more sensitive or more honest man'. Bruner speaks of himself as a 'functionalist', that is, one who seeks to investigate the mind by studying the human organism as an entity functioning in its environment. Further, a human being may be thought of as 'an information processor, thinker and creator'. The role of the teacher in Bruner's cognitive theory is seen as vital to the maintenance of our culture which requires the transmission of knowledge to the young. 'Knowledge, we know now as never before, is power... Let knowledge as it appears in our education be placed within a context of action and commitment.'

Bruner has maintained his opposition to behaviourism and, in particular, to those 'who extrapolate from rabbits and pigeons to the human being'. He rejects the relevance of operant conditioning for the processes of instruction. Skinner's reply suggests that Bruner has not understood operant conditioning well enough to see its relevance for learning.

Bruner: the background

Bruner was born in America in 1916 and graduated from Duke University and Harvard, where his experimental work in psychology convinced him that the effective instruction of human beings involves leading them through sequences of statements of problems or aspects of knowledge which cumulatively increase the ability 'to group, transform, and transfer what is being learned'. He became professor of psychology at Harvard in 1952 and established and directed the influential Centre for Cognitive Studies. In 1973 he was appointed professor of experimental psychology at Oxford. Bruner's special interest in the craft of teaching led him to a long-term programme of empirical research in schools and colleges and to a lasting interest in the role of the teacher and the relationship between insight, understanding and competence.

The literature

Among Bruner's many writings, the following texts will be of particular interest to college tutors: *A Study of Thinking* (1990), dealing with the formation and use of concepts; *The Process of Education* (1960), reporting a congress on teaching for understanding; *On Knowing* (1962), essays on the phenomenon of human knowledge; *Toward a Theory of Instruction* (1962), perhaps Bruner's most influential text; *Studies in Cognitive Growth* (1966), an examination of development and 'meaningful teaching'; *The Relevance of Education* (1973), learning skills and educational strategies; *Actual Minds, Possible Worlds* (1986), an exploration of the significance of preparing for change.

The essence of learning and development

Learning is viewed by Bruner in terms beyond the mere acquisition of knowledge; he sees its end as the creation of the developed human being. The institutions in which formal learning takes place – the schools and colleges – are responsible for the important task of 'amplification of intellectual skills'. That amplification involves instruction concerning the place of the student in the culture of his or her society; indeed, intelligence is seen by Bruner as, 'to a great extent, the internalisation of tools' provided by that culture. Cultural variations produce variations in modes of thinking so that a student's cognitive growth will be influenced directly by social patterns.

Students should be trained to develop their capacities to the full. Understanding of principles should be developed if students are to be given confidence in their capabilities. They must be taught *how* to analyze problems. What students should be learning is not 'particular performances', but *competence*, and central to the attainment of that end is the acquisition of *correct modes of thinking*. Bruner's emphasis on understanding of principles mirrors an earlier statement by Whitehead:

> *Whatever be the detail with which you cram your students, the chance of their meeting in after-life exactly that detail is almost infinitesimal; and if they do meet it, they will probably have forgotten what you taught them about it. The really useful training yields a comprehension of a few general principles with a thorough grounding in the way they apply to a variety of concrete details. In subsequent practice the student will have forgotten your particular details; but he will remember to apply principles to immediate circumstances.*[2]

Bruner's cognitive-development theory is concerned with how what one wishes to teach can best be learned; it takes into account both learning and development.

Bruner and the learning process

The cognitive school of psychology is concerned with the 'building of a mental bridge' between the stimulus and response in the S-R process. Bruner emphasizes the role of perception in that process.[3] Perception is the operation by which the learner interprets or gives some meaning to sensory material and that 'meaning' will result from the context of the stimulus (in the learner and his or her environment) and the learner's past experiences with similar types of sensory stimulation. The brain, according to Bruner, selects some stimuli related to the learner's needs, values, attitudes, etc. Stimuli which are of a threatening type are ignored. The process is named 'perceptual defence'. Sensory experience is organized by the learner's brain in relation to past experiences so as to interpret the current situation. As the result of 'fixation' the recurrence of a stimulus is accompanied by the recurrence of the same type of perceptual experience produced on its previous appearances.

Learning is a cognitive process involving the learner *acquiring* new information, *transforming* his state of existing knowledge and *checking* the adequacy of that state of knowledge against the demands of new situations. (In Popper's words:[4] 'Knowledge is always a modification of earlier knowledge ... [it] goes back, ultimately, to inborn knowledge'.) We learn best, not by committing a body of knowledge to mind, but by 'participating in the process that makes possible the establishment of knowledge'. *Knowledge is a process, not a product.* The acquisition of knowledge is an active process and depends for its effectiveness on the learner relating incoming information to previously acquired frames of reference. Learners gradually acquire internal models, giving them a pattern of meaning for their experiences so that they are able to extrapolate on the basis of that pattern. They construct hypotheses to explain incoming information and test them so as to produce meaningful interpretations of reality.

Learners construct models of the external world and those models will be determined largely by *the culture of society*. An adequate model will not only explain objective reality, but will predict 'how the world might be'. The models become expectancies allowing the learner to make short-cuts and leaps from partial evidence, reflecting the human tendency to categorize. The construction of categories involves the learner's ability to create strategies, that is, sequences of mental events related to goals. Inherent in any strategy are three factors. The first is the *informational situation* which will determine whether more information needs to be gathered by the learner before he arrives at a conclusion. The second factor is the *certainty of cognition*, that is, the intensity of the thinking needed to arrive at a conclusion. The third factor is the *general consequence of failure*, that is, the 'risk' involved in the result of cognition. These factors interact to produce a learner's strategy of movement towards a learning goal. (Gagné[5] criticizes this concept of strategies. To know a strategy is not even a substantial part of what is needed. The learner cannot solve problems effectively until he has acquired 'masses of organized intellectual skills'.)

Growth in learning capacity is *not*, according to Bruner, a gradual accretion of associations or S-R connections; it is 'a matter of spurts and rests... The spurts ahead in growth seem to be touched off when certain capacities begin to develop'. These spurts do not necessarily depend on the learner's age, but rather on his or her ability to organize incoming information within frames of reference and models of reality. *The development of that ability is one of the teacher's principal tasks*. But the difficulties of this task should not be underestimated. Butterfield, the historian of science, reminds us:

> *Of all forms of mental activity, the most difficult to induce even in the minds of the young, who may be presumed not to have lost their flexibility, is the art of handling the same bundle of data as before, but placing them in a new system of relations with one another by giving them a different framework.*[6]

One of Bruner's most controversial statements is that 'any subject can be taught effectively in some intellectually honest form to any child at any stage of development'. It is merely a matter of 'representing the structure of that subject in terms of the child's way of viewing things', that is, on an intuitive, experiential level; the idea can then be developed and redeveloped as the learner matures intellectually; a 'spiral sequence of learning' is then produced by a periodical recycling of the same ideas at greater levels of complexity. Ausubel has attacked this statement as ignoring the fact that some abstractions are so inherently complex and difficult that they cannot be made understandable to persons below a certain level of cognitive maturity. In a pointed criticism of Bruner's statement, Tyler[7] asks: 'Do common experience and observation not convince us of the impossibility of teaching such a class of responses as "solving linear equations" to a neonate?' (Bruner's response is that he had phrased his statement so as to suggest the possibility of teaching 'meaningful aspects of any subject' at certain age levels.)

The purposes of the educational process

In Bruner's view, education is concerned with the intensification of cognitive skills related to the principles and needs of the community's culture; it should be linked closely to an understanding and development of those 'technologies and their tools' which are a vital part of cultural expression. The purposes of education may be categorized as follows.

1. The development of the student's confidence in his or her innate capacities and their potential for development. This involves a curriculum which will encourage the student to explore strategies of learning through problem-solving.

2. The development of the student's confidence in his or her ability to solve problems of a new type through 'use of the mind'. The development of understanding and a knowledge of transforming one's powers of cognition will be of much importance.

3. The motivation of the student to operate on his or her own with confidence. Location of 'the form of a problem' is important and this requires the study of techniques of interpretation.

4. The development of 'economy in the use of the mind'. This will necessitate training directed at the skills needed to search for 'relevance and structure', i.e. 'reflective learning'.

5. The development of intellectual honesty in the student. It is the task of the teacher to insist upon rigour and self-discipline in the attainment of goals in the various disciplines of our culture.

A theory of instruction

A theory of instruction appropriate for our day and our type of society must be, according to Bruner, both prescriptive and normative. It must involve the enunciation of rules concerning effectiveness in attaining knowledge and must provide for the evaluation of modes of teaching and learning. Criteria for instruction must be considered. Such a theory can be built around five essential features.

1. It must specify the experiences which will most effectively predispose students to learn. Effective learning will involve a rigorous 'exploration of alternatives', leading to 'learning how to learn'.

2. It must specify ways of structuring knowledge so that optimal comprehension might be attained by students. A general understanding of the fundamental structure of a subject necessitates grasping its inner significance by comprehension of basic, generalized principles, so that knowledge that is of significance can be extracted from information that is less so.

3. It must specify the optimal sequences of presentation of the material to be learned. Subject matters have their own appropriate 'forms of representation', allowing knowledge of their principles to be converted into comprehensible structures.

4. It must specify 'the nature and pacing of reinforcement' in the processes of teaching and learning. This involves examining and correcting the learner during the instructional process in a fashion which will make it possible for him or her to

take over the corrective function, thus avoiding the danger of establishing in the learner a permanent dependence 'upon a scaffolding of reward and a rewarder'. (*This will necessitate appropriate feedback of results to the student.* It should come at that point in a problem-solving episode 'when the student is comparing the results of this try-out with some criterion of what he or she seeks to achieve'.)

5. It must seek to take into account the fact that a curriculum ought to reflect the nature of knowledge and 'the nature of the knower and the knowledge-getting process'.

Bruner's work and the teacher

Interpreting the cultural patterns of society for the learner and assisting him or her to achieve mastery of the processes inherent in creative thinking are the tasks of the teacher, according to Bruner. Students must be taught in a manner which allows them to comprehend single instances in terms of broad generalizations and principles. Bruner stresses that the student learning physics 'is a physicist, and it is easier for him to learn physics behaving like a physicist than doing something else'. The class teacher has the responsibility of ensuring that methods of teaching are *realistic* in that they allow *discovery activity*; purely expository teaching on its own is of little value, according to Bruner, in helping a student to acquire the capacity to think creatively and critically.

Bruner's call for 'discovery learning' (or, as he occasionally refers to it, 'inquiry training') reflects his belief that 'the curriculum of a subject should be determined by the most fundamental understanding that can be achieved of the underlying principles that give *structure* to that subject'. Teaching will be most productive where the subject matter is 'gutted' so that its bare bones – its structural elements – are revealed and made a foundation for the acquisition of principles. A student who knows the *principles* of a discipline has the power to investigate and solve problems within its terms; additionally, the student is more likely to remember information associated with these principles.

In discovering the 'meaning' of principles, a student is learning concepts and relationships. Bruner suggests that the activity of discovering has four advantages. (These should be of interest to the further education lecturer involved, in particular, with first-level and foundation courses.) First, there is a growth in 'intellectual potency' – the student acquires the ability to develop strategies in approaching and analyzing patterns in his or her environment in an organized manner. Secondly, intrinsic motivation becomes a preferred alternative to extrinsic rewards – the student achieves satisfaction from discovering solutions on his or her own. Thirdly, the student who has mastered the techniques of discovery learning is able to apply them to the solution of real problems outside the classroom. Fourthly, improvements in memory seem to be associated with the organization of one's knowledge – retrieval of information stored in the memory becomes easier where the student has organized his knowledge in terms of his own system.

Building on Bruner's views, Taba[8] outlines some general steps in discovery learning. First, learners should be confronted with a problem that initiates a 'feeling of bafflement'. No important generalizations should be offered by the teacher at this stage; learners must be encouraged to explore the problem for themselves. Next, they should be prompted to utilize previously acquired knowledge so as to understand new patterns and structures from which will emerge solutions to the problem facing them. They should then be given an opportunity to demonstrate, in relation to other problems, the principles they have now acquired. In this way the teacher has provided the conditions facilitating the learner's discovery of 'organizing principles'.

Mastery of specifics is essential if the student is to make progress and it is the teacher's task to ensure such mastery. 'Lower-order regularities' must be mastered if there is to be movement towards higher-order learning. Students must be given an opportunity to master specifics by developing skills related to immediate problems in which their knowledge may be put to use. The 'exploration of alternatives' (i.e. 'diversity of learning') must be part of the instructional process and it should be linked with a 'general understanding of the subject matter'. The acquisition of a generalized set of basic ideas is an important aim of classroom instruction; indeed, according to Bruner, one of the true tests of learning is whether the student has grasped, and can use, 'the generic code' he or she has been taught. Speed of learning, resistance to forgetting, transfer of learning, creation of ability to generalize and to create new hypotheses are some of the criteria of instruction. A curriculum built on rudiments acquired at an early age, moving upwards and circling back to previous understanding, is essential for the successful structuring of subject matter. Such a curriculum ought to be built 'around the great issues, principles and values that a society deems worthy of the continual concern of its members'.[9] Development and redevelopment of the learners' capacities, so that they are able to deal with problems at advancing levels of complexity, are the prerequisites of successful learning and this necessitates appropriate planning of instruction in the classroom.

Bruner argues also in favour of students being given training 'in recognizing the plausibility of guesses'. Educated guesses, which may possess the elements of an 'intuitive leap' are not to be discouraged. To repress guessing is, in effect, to check some of the cognitive processes inherent in discovery.

From the variety of teaching techniques suggested by Bruner, Dembo[10] selects four which, taken together, could constitute an effective teaching model for many college courses. First, teach the *basic structure* of the subject, emphasizing concepts, fundamental principles and relationships. Next, experiment with discovery learning techniques so that students are motivated and assisted in the acquisition and retention of principles. Thirdly, consider the advisability of commencing instructional periods with a problem that calls for the utilization of previously acquired knowledge in order to assist students in the search for solutions at a new level of knowledge. Finally, pitch the instruction at a level appropriate to a student's overall cognitive functioning so that concept formation is encouraged.

On the teacher's role in reinforcement of learning, Bruner is categorical. He calls for a 'de-emphasis of extrinsic rewards'. Intrinsic rewards should be emphasized: the teacher's task is to arrange instruction so that there is a challenge to students to exercise their mental powers fully and to heighten their inner sense of accomplishment. The danger of creating dependence upon rewards is to be avoided. In the absence of external rewards, students need continuous knowledge of their progress; this involves effective feedback. 'Knowledge of results should come at that point in a problem-solving episode when the person is comparing the results of his try-out with some criterion of what he seeks to achieve.'

Instruction, Bruner reminds the teacher, 'is, after all, an effort to assist or shape growth'. It is the responsibility of the teacher to seek to understand growth as development, and to link this understanding to an appropriate theory of knowledge and instruction.

Notes and references: Bruner

1. See generally: *Introduction to Cognitive Studies* by A Asham (Routledge, 1997); *The Conscious Mind* by D Chalmers (OUP, 1996); *The Idea of Consciousness* by M Bennett (Harvard, 1997); *An Introduction to Teaching: Psychological Perspectives* (ed) C Desfarges (Blackwell, 1995); *In the Theatre of Consciousness* by BJ Baars (OUP, 1997).
2. *The Aims of Education* (Macmillan, 1929).
3. See 'On perceptual readiness' in *Psychological Review* (1957, 64); 'An approach to social perception' in *Current Trends in Social Psychology* by J Bruner and L Postman (Pittsburgh UP, 1948).
4. See *The Self and Its Brain* by K Popper and J Eccles (Routledge & Kegan Paul, 1984). See also *Evolution of the Brain: Creation of the Self* by J Eccles (Routledge, 1989).
5. *The Conditions of Learning* (Holt Saunders, 1985).
6. *The Origins of Modern Science* (Macmillan, 1957).
7. 'Issues related to readiness' in *Theories of Learning and Instruction* (Chicago UP, 1964).
8. 'Learning by discovery' in *School Journal* (1963, 3).
9. 'Beyond the information given' by Bruner in *Studies in the Psychology of Knowing* (Norton, 1973).
10. *Teaching for Learning* (Goodyear, 1981).

3. Attitudes and Attitude Change

Nicky Hayes

We all frequently talk about our own and other people's *attitudes,* but what exactly do we mean by the word? What are our attitudes, and how do they affect how we deal with the world around us?

The concept of attitudes

Definitions

There have been a number of different attempts to define attitudes. Fishbein & Ajzen (1975), for example, defined them as 'learned predispositions to respond in a consistently favourable or unfavourable way towards a given object, person, or event'. This definition emphasises three features of attitudes: firstly, they are learned; secondly, they are consistent; and thirdly, they are concerned with favourable or unfavourable responses.

A similar emphasis is present in the definition suggested by Krech, Crutchfield & Ballachey in 1962: 'Attitudes are enduring systems of positive or negative evaluations, emotional feelings, and pro and con action tendencies with respect to social objectives.' In addition, though, this definition emphasises the way attitudes are concerned with doing – with taking action of some kind.

Other definitions of attitudes emphasise how they prepare us for action – making us more likely to act in certain ways than in others. So, for instance, the definition put forward by Osgood, Suci & Tannenbaum in 1957 was 'attitudes are predispositions to respond, but are distinguished from other states of readiness in that they predispose towards an evaluative response.' According to this definition, an attitude is a bit like a mental 'set', but with underlying values.

Attitudes and behaviour

Whichever definition we adopt, we can see that an attitude consists of more than just a set of ideas about something. In particular, attitudes are thought to have a link with how we act – it is believed they underlie behaviour. But do they?

In one famous investigation into whether attitudes and behaviour are consistent, LaPière (1934) showed how the attitudes people say they have may be quite different from the attitudes implied by their behaviour. LaPière and two Chinese friends travelled across America, staying at hotels and eating in restaurants. Over 90% of places accepted the customers without demur, even though anti-Chinese prejudice was a major racial bias in American society at that time. But six months later, LaPière contacted those same hotels and restaurants across America to ask whether they accepted Chinese guests, and almost all the hoteliers said they did not.

The suggestion, then, is that the attitudes which people express don't necessarily allow us to predict how they will act. But Ajzen (1988) argued this was misleading, and believed people do act consistently with their attitudes in general; but those attitudes can vary in terms of how global or specific they are. In the case of LaPière's study, the hoteliers were being asked a very general question which revealed their prejudiced attitudes; but when the three researchers actually turned up on the doorstep, they were faced with a very specific situation involving two individuals rather than 'Chinese people' in general. It was this difference in focus, Ajzen argued, which led to the apparent discrepancy between attitudes and behaviour.

In addition, Ajzen pointed out, during investigations of consistency between attitudes and beliefs, people may be faced with a conflict between two contradictory attitudes. So, for instance, the racism of the hotelier may have conflicted with the hotelier's belief that customers must be served in order for the business to be successful. Ajzen regarded many of the studies into attitude consistency as being naive, in that they didn't take social pressures and other attitudes into account.

When we are studying attitudes, it rapidly becomes apparent they are complex things which can operate on a number of different levels. Attitudes are often described as having three dimensions, each of which contributes to the whole:

- The *cognitive dimension* – concerned with the beliefs and ideas which the person holds towards the attitude target.
- The *affective dimension* – concerned with the way the person feels about the attitude target; in other words, their emotions or emotional responses.
- The *conative,* or *behavioural dimension* – concerned with the individual's tendency to act, or to take action with respect to the attitude target.

While definitions vary in the emphasis they put on each of these three dimensions, they are all significant in the development of the attitude as a whole.

Attitudes, values and beliefs

In 1975 Fishbein & Ajzen argued that we need to distinguish between attitudes and beliefs; and the differences lie in the emotional dimension involved. Essentially, according to Fishbein & Ajzen, the beliefs we hold are relatively neutral: they are simply statements which are believed to be true. But the attitudes we hold are evaluative: they indicate how we feel about the matter concerned. Eiser (1983) discussed how attitude statements can often appear to be statements about beliefs, until we look carefully at the words used to describe them. The emotive language people use when describing something is often a key indicator to their underlying attitude.

Another important distinction we need to make when thinking about attitudes concerns values. Values are the consistent, personal assumptions we make which underpin our attitudes. They are concerned with general principles, like moral rights and wrongs, or social desirability. Because our personal values and principles are the standards by which we judge others and our own behaviour, they are closely linked with attitudes. In most cases, attitudes can be seen to derive directly from a set of underlying values held by an individual.

However, there are also cases of individuals espousing a set of attitudes which are inconsistent with their personal values. For example, Arendt (1963) discussed how Eichmann, the Nazi official responsible for organising the transport of millions of Jews to concentration camps, did not have particularly strong anti-Jewish attitudes, and in fact made some effort to protect particular Jewish people he knew. His support of Nazi ideology came from the social norms with which he was surrounded rather than his internal values. But none the less, he acted in accord with socially expressed attitudes, causing millions of deaths, and his personal values were (quite rightly) regarded as irrelevant at his trial.

This may be quite an extreme example, but it is important to realise that the attitudes implied by an individual's behaviour do not inevitably express personal beliefs. However, this doesn't mean that beliefs are unimportant; rather, we have to take responsibility for our actions as well as our beliefs.

What are attitudes for?

Smith, Bruner & White (1964) draw a distinction between the opinions people hold, and those they actually express. They see the expression of attitudes as involving social strategies, and as operating under social constraints; so although these expressions are related to the attitudes people actually hold, they may not be precisely the same thing. But the attitudes people hold, in their view, are the main tools we use to deal with reality.

Smith, Bruner & White argue that attitudes serve three distinct functions: object appraisal, social adjustment, and externalisation.

Object appraisal is the way attitudes can guide our reactions towards objects and features in our environment, so we don't need to work out how we will react to them again each time we encounter them. So, for instance, we develop an attitude towards something we have found harmful in the past, and this means we will avoid it in the future without having to learn about its harmful nature all over again.

Attitudes are also involved in *social adjustment*. Obviously, expressing opinions may serve a number of social functions, including confirming social relationships and helping group cohesiveness. Smith, Bruner & White suggested that holding opinions serves a social adjustment function too, in that it aids affiliation with social groups – if I hold an opinion similar to those held by members of one of my reference groups, it is my way of saying 'I am like them'. This also applies to negative reference groups – someone may hold a diametrically opposed view to members of a social group in order to emphasise their differences.

So Smith and colleagues see the holding of an opinion as aiding social identification, which is an important – some would say central – part of being human and taking part in human societies.

The third function of an attitude which Smith, Bruner & White identified is *externalisation*. Externalisation is concerned with the matching up of unconscious motivations or inner states with something going on in the individual's immediate environment. This matching, which is often entirely unconscious, results in the individual developing an attitude towards the external object, thus allowing some of the inner conflict or state to be channelled into a form of expression.

So, for instance, someone who experiences inner conflict as a result of a lack of stable relationships with others may express a deep scepticism about the institution of marriage. Their attitude towards marriage as an institution allows them to express some of their inner feelings about relationships. The essential idea here, according to Smith *et al.* is that an external object is treated as if it were relevant to an internal problem.

Smith, Bruner & White suggested that the interplay of these three functions of attitudes serves several different functions which might explain why, at times, attitudes can be so resistant to change. The researchers believe everyone has a constant drive towards understanding the world better, which would normally result in modification of attitudes. But inner demands and anxieties may mean the person feels threatened by too great a change at any one time. So attitude change is easier if either:

1. it takes place a little at a time, and/or with attitudes which are peripheral rather than central to a person's functions; or
2. the person is in a state which is reasonably free of disruptive inner anxieties.

Smith and colleagues also point out that the development of opinion has to happen within the information available to an individual. Since opinions develop as a result of the individual's striving to make sense of the world, a world which presents only one view is not likely to result in what the researchers called 'maturation of opinions'. But if the individual is faced with multiple views of the world – different sources of information – then as they seek to make sense out of it, they will develop and mature their own ideas. In the researchers' view it is therefore important to have multiple viewpoints in society, if we are to encourage its members to adopt a mature approach...

Changing attitudes

Perhaps understandably, a considerable amount of research into attitudes has concentrated on how they can be changed – how we can persuade other people to take a different view. Research of this kind has encompassed not just how to reduce prejudices, ... but also ... cognitive aspects of attitude change, and the type of persuasion involved in advertising. And advertising, of course, is really all about persuading people that to buy this or that product or use this or that service is a good idea.

Cognitive balance and cognitive dissonance

Heider (1944) believed people tend to aim for *cognitive balance* or consistency, preferring that the different attitudes they hold should each be consistent with one another. Inconsistency between attitudes, Heider argued, produced a state of cognitive imbalance which was inherently stressful; and people would act to reduce the tension produced, either by changing the situation or changing their cognitions.

Mower-White (1977) asked subjects to judge situations involving triads of people (e.g. Jane likes Sally, Sally likes Elizabeth, Elizabeth dislikes Jane). The ratings were estimates of how pleasant or unpleasant the situation would be. Half of the situations referred directly to the subject, using the pronoun 'you'. The rest were more impersonal, referring to other people. Mower-White found it was the personal involvement of the subjects which counted: if the situation concerned other people, subjects were not worried about lack of balance. But when it referred to them personally, they rated balanced situations as 'pleasant' and unbalanced ones as 'unpleasant'.

Newcomb (1968) suggested a cognitive imbalance would only produce tension if it were highly relevant. So, for example, if you dislike someone you have met, and whom your friend likes, it wouldn't matter unless it was going to affect your life in some way. If the person lived a long way away, and your friend only met them when they went on holiday, you'd be unlikely to feel tension at the imbalance. But if they moved next door to your friend, and were likely to be socialising with both of you, the situation could produce tension.

Basing his work largely on Heider's ideas, Leon Festinger (1957) proposed that *cognitive dissonance* is a major source of attitude change. Cognitive dissonance occurs when we find our attitudes or beliefs contradict one another – either because they aren't balanced, as in Heider's theory, or because they are in direct conflict with one another.

We deal with the resulting tension in one of two ways: by changing one of the attitudes; or by adding additional ones which will allow us to interpret the situation differently.

In one famous study, Festinger, Riecken & Schachter (1956) performed a participant observation of a religious cult. The sect believed a major US city was about to be destroyed by flood – except for the members of the cult, who would be rescued by a flying saucer. Cult members sold their possessions and went to a hill outside the city, waiting for the event. Festinger and colleagues found that, when the predictions failed to come true, the group coped with the cognitive dissonance thus produced by adding an additional belief: the city had been saved as a result of the prayers of the cult.

In another study, Festinger & Carlsmith (1959) asked subjects to perform a very boring task for an hour. The task involved putting pegs into holes in a peg-board, and giving them quarter-turns. When the hour was up they were asked how they had found it, and all of them said it was boring. Then they were asked to introduce the next subject to the experiment, telling them the task was fun and interesting to do. The subjects were paid for doing this, but for one group the pay was very low – only $1 – while for the other group the level of pay was much higher – $20. After

41

everything was completed, they were asked again what they thought of the experiment.

Festinger & Carlsmith found the subjects who'd been paid $20 hadn't changed their attitudes towards the task. But those who'd been paid only $1 rated the task as very much more enjoyable than previously; and enjoyed it more than the other group. Festinger argued this arose from cognitive dissonance. The highly paid group could justify lying to the new subjects on the grounds they had done it for the money. But the low-paid group hadn't earned enough to make lying worthwhile, so they had changed their attitudes to reduce the dissonance between how they felt and what they told the new subjects.

Festinger argued that cognitive dissonance is a major factor in inducing attitude change. But people with strong feelings on an issue are often highly resistant to information which contradicts their beliefs, and they will tend to defend against it. They may simply ignore the information; or they may distort it so it becomes consistent with their beliefs. The distortion can take a number of forms:

1. discrediting the source of the information;
2. re-analysing the information so it is seen as having different implications;
3. being highly selective about which bits of information they will notice or recall.

People are often entirely unconscious of how selective they are being. For example, Postman, Bruner & McGinnies (1948) demonstrated how, when shown a list of words very rapidly, people are more likely to recognise words with highly valued or pleasant associations, and less likely to recognise those with unpleasant or taboo associations. Their attitudes act as a kind of 'filter', screening out words which would be disturbing.

References

Ajzen I (1988) *Attitudes, personality and behaviour* Open University Press

Arendt H (1963) *Eichmann in Jerusalem: a report on banality of evil* Viking Press

Eiser JR (1983) 'From attributions to behaviour' in M Hewstone (ed) *Attribution theory: social and functional extensions* Basil Blackwell

Festinger L (1957) *A theory of cognitive dissonance* Row, Peterson

Festinger L & Carlsmith LM (1959) 'Cognitive consequences of forced compliance' *Journal of Abnormal and Social Psychology* (58), pp203–210

Festinger L, Riecken HW & Schachter S (1956) *When prophecy fails* University of Minneapolis Press

Fishbein M & Ajzen I (1975) *Attitude intention and behaviour: an introduction to theory and research* Addison-Wesley

Heider F (1944) 'Social perception and phenomenal causality' *Psychological Review* (51), pp358–374

Krech D, Crutchfield RS & Ballachey EL (1962) *The individual in society* McGraw Hill

LaPière RT (1934) 'Attitudes and actions' *Social Forces* (13), pp230–237

Mower-White CJ (1977) 'A limitation of balance theory: the effects of identification with a member of a triad' *European Journal of Social Psychology* (7), pp111–116

Newcomb TM (1968) 'Interpersonal balance' in RP Abelson *et al.* (eds) *Theories of cognitive consistency: a source book* Rand McNally

Osgood CE, Suci CJ & Tannenbaum PH (1957) *The measurement of meaning* University of Illinois Press

Postman L, Bruner JS & McGinnies F (1948) 'Personal values as selective factors in perception' *Journal of Abnormal and Social Psychology* (43), pp142–154

Smith MB, Bruner JS & White RW (1964) 'Opinions and personality' in J Murphy *et al.* (eds) (1984) *Dialogues and debates in social psychology* Lawrence Erlbaum

Part Two – Student Diversity

It can be argued that one of the debates which dominated the closing years of the 20th century in relation to post-16 education and training concerned issues of access and participation. Indeed, 'widening the participation' of so-called under-represented groups of learners was at the centre of some of the most significant policy reviews and analyses in the 1980s and 1990s which have impacted upon further, adult and higher education and training in the UK.

As a confirmation of the official concern about under-representation, the Secretary of State for Education and Employment, David Blunkett, argued, in relation specifically to access to HE:

> ...*relative participation rates of different socioeconomic groups, as well as those with disabilities, and some ethnic minority groups, remain* **strikingly and unacceptably low**. (emphasis added)

> (Blunkett, 2000)

This observation echoes those which had been voiced earlier in the Kennedy report into widening participation in further education (FEFC, 1997) and the report of Dearing's national inquiry into higher education (Dearing, 1997).

Strategies in response to the expressions of government commitment to improving the participation rates did indeed emerge during the 1990s. These included: attempts to raise achievement levels in schools and colleges; a reform of the 16 plus qualifications at advanced level; proposals for two-year foundation degrees; and numerous financial initiatives aimed at rewarding institutions which have successfully 'widened the participation of under-represented groups' (Blunkett, 2000).

Whilst analysis of these reviews and the strategies and policies that emanate from them is beyond the scope of this Reader the context set by such initiatives cannot be ignored in any consideration of the principles and practices involved in teaching in the post-school sector. What this Part of the Reader aims to do, therefore, is to consider issues associated with student diversity as it affects the practitioner in PCET.

The first contribution considers the ways in which students are psychologically different from each other in terms of their approach to learning, and how these individual differences can affect the teaching and learning process. James Hartley explores the relationship between cognitive styles, learning strategies and preferences, and gives some indication of how a tutor can best respond to these acknowledged psychological differences. The practitioner who is aware of such differences is more likely to be able to recognise and respond to the needs of previously 'excluded' groups of learners.

The section on cultural diversity draws, in contrast, on a sociological tradition which has concerned itself with the very issues of access and participation in education for the past 30 years. In this section, the nature of the sociological inquiry is established and a key concept – culture – is explored. The section on access and opportunity then assesses some of the detailed arguments in relation to access, achievement and participation, and analyses social variables such as social class, gender, sexuality, race and ethnicity, and disability. In each of the sections various sociological explanations of differential achievement are explored and compared. The intention here is to go beyond a description of 'what is' the situation to explanations of 'why' this continues.

In conclusion, by asking why and exploring the explanations we should be able to arrive at an understanding of the complexity of the phenomenon – student diversity and adult learning. If we teachers and trainers are to recognise, accommodate, utilise and celebrate difference, we will be more able to develop effective and supportive learning situations for *all* our learners.

References

Blunkett D (2000) 'Reaching out to make society just' *Times Higher Education Supplement* May 12th

Dearing R (1997) *Higher education in the learning society – the report of the National Committee of Inquiry into Higher Education* HMSO

FEFC (1997) *Learning works: widening participation in FE – the Kennedy Report* Further Education Funding Council

4. Individual Differences and Learning

James Hartley

This chapter is concerned with differences between individuals and how they can affect teaching and learning. In a lecture situation, although everyone is different, the lecturer has to proceed as though everyone is the same – making an occasional acknowledgement to sub-groups in the audience. Yet the opposite viewpoint – that no two learners are alike – poses equally difficult constraints on teachers. Individuals can really only be catered for in one-to-one instruction. However, in some situations – in classrooms and tutorials, for example – tutors can explore (and exploit) individual differences in ways that, it is to be hoped, will help all the participants learn.

Table 1 (overleaf) lists different kinds of individual differences related to learning and studying under four headings. These I call:

- *fundamental differences* – fundamental in the sense that these are very hard to alter;
- *cognitive styles* – these are ways in which different individuals characteristically approach different cognitive tasks;
- *learning strategies* – these are ways in which individuals more consciously select methods of approach; and
- *preferences* – these are less serious ways in which individuals differ.

Research has been conducted with all of the individual differences (and others) that I have listed in Table 1. Clearly, in this chapter I do not have sufficient space to cover them all or, indeed, all of the research on any particular one. So I have chosen to discuss one characteristic example from each of the four groups, and to provide (in Table 1) references to recent papers on each of the differences listed.

Fundamental differences

As can be seen from the kinds of differences listed in Table 1, this first category describes differences that are very hard to change. That being said, of course, although you cannot change things like age and sex, there is much debate about the influences of such variables on learning and studying. At university level, for instance, prior experiences in connection with these two variables are bound to affect how people learn. Here, as a characteristic example of a fundamental difference between people, I shall consider sex differences in intellectual abilities.

Sex differences in intellectual abilities

In the 1980s the picture that was drawn concerning differences between the sexes in terms of intellectual abilities was relatively clear-cut. Although it was always acknowledged that vast oversimplifications were being made, it was considered that males and females did not differ greatly on intelligence, that boys were better at spatial tasks, and that girls were better at verbal ones. These views were based largely on the influential book written by Maccoby & Jacklin in 1974. This book set out, by reviewing as much of the research literature as possible, to consider the evidence for the views and beliefs that people had about the differences between males and females.

Fundamental differences
    Age (Sutherland, 1997)
    Culture (McNamara & Harris, 1997)
    Ability (Wong *et al.* 1995)
    Sex (Hayes & Richardson, 1995)
    Introversion/extraversion (Eysenck & Eysenck, 1985)
    Motivation (Abouserie, 1995)
    Anxiety (Zeidner, 1996)

Cognitive styles and ways of thinking
    Convergent/divergent (Hartley & Greggs, 1997)
    Reflexive/impulsive (Goldman & Flake, 1996)
    Field dependent/independent (Liu & Reed, 1994)
    Visualisers/verbalisers (Kirby, 1993)
    Abstract/concrete/active/reflective (Willcoxson & Prosser, 1996)
    Locus of control (Millar & Irving, 1995)

Learning strategies
    Deep/surface approaches (Sadler-Smith, 1996)
    Serialists/holists (Paterson & Rosbottom, 1995)
    Focusers/scanners (Santostefano, 1985)
    Various study methods (Chalmers & Fuller, 1996)

Preferences
    Prior knowledge and interest (Tobias, 1994)
    Morning/evening persons (Greenwood, 1995)
    Seating positions (Burda & Brooks, 1996)

Note: Jonassen & Grabowski (1993) provide additional references to studies on most of these variables, and Riding & Rayner (1997) provide a recent work on cognitive styles.

Table 1 Some examples of individual differences (and related studies)

Maccoby & Jacklin's approach was to summarise the known evidence using the tools then available. Since that time the evidence has mushroomed, and newer statistical tools, such as meta-analysis, have become available for handling it. This newer approach has indicated that the conclusions listed above are oversimplifications. Archer (1996) writes, 'Increased quantification ... brought the realisation that many of the sex differences that had been extensively discussed and argued over were relatively small in terms of overall effect size'. Not only were these effect-sizes seen to be small, but the arguments about interpreting them became more sophisticated. Halpern's (1992) *Sex Differences in Cognitive Abilities* provides a good beginning for readers interested in pursuing these issues in more detail.

Archer (1996) goes on to point out that social contexts are important in determining what appear to be sex differences. He cites studies showing that, for example, 'If the *same* task is presented to boys or girls as *either* a measure of needlework *or* of electronics, the effect of the labelling is to reverse the direction of sex difference in the performance' (emphasis added). The significance of this point of view for this particular chapter is to suggest that the differences between the sexes in an academic context – say, in how many men and women students enrol for engineering – are a function of how they perceive engineering, rather than a consequence of biological differences between them.

Many people also think – because there is today less sex-typed socialisation in the home, the school and the media than in the past – that this accounts for the fact that many of the differences that were once found between the sexes on measures of intellectual abilities have now begun to disappear. Halpern (1992) points to the difficulties of drawing such firm conclusions on issues such as these. It is quite likely, for instance, that the people taking part in studies of sex differences at different time periods will also differ in all manner of other ways.

None the less it is true that these recent social changes have had a remarkable effect on the composition of students attending higher education in the UK. Less than twenty years ago, nearly twice as many men as women went to university, and three times as many did postgraduate work. Today the ratios are much more evenly balanced. However, once they are at university, do women do as well as men? And does this vary for different subject matters?

For many years, the achievement of men at university has been slightly more widespread than that of women; that is to say, there have been proportionally more men with very good degrees and more men with very poor degrees than women, and that there have been proportionally more women with middle-quality degrees than men. This generalisation is supported by the data shown in Table 2, which shows the percentage of full-time men and women students achieving different degree classes in the United Kingdom in 1995. Such findings have been reported in other different, earlier studies of full-time students by, for example, Rudd (1984) and Davies & Harré (1989). The current findings in Table 2 are, therefore, of considerable interest, for they present much the same picture despite the fact that there have been massive changes in the university system in the UK – such as the increase in the number of universities, the increase in the number of students within them, the increase in the number of modular-based systems (as opposed to the old-fashioned 'finals' where the students' degree classes depended almost entirely upon work carried out and examined in the final year) and the increase in the number of women and mature students.

There have, of course, been a variety of explanations proffered for such findings, and the debate can get quite heated (see Clarke, 1988; Rudd, 1988). Some people (e.g.

Rudd) prefer to explain such findings at the top end on the basis of differences in intelligence or ability between the two sexes.

Degree class					
Full time	*1st*	*2.1*	*2.2*	*3rd*	Pass
Men (N = 104,654)	8	38	37	7	10
Women (N = 106,553)	6	47	36	4	7
(Source: Adapted from figures provided by the Higher Education Statistical Agency)					

Table 2   Percentage of full-time men and women students achieving different degree classes in 1995

Others (e.g. Clarke) prefer a more social explanation – looking at issues of sex discrimination, and how the data differ for different subject combinations. Thus, for example, it appears that there are more first-class degrees in science subjects than in arts subjects and that more men students study the sciences than women (Tomlinson & Macfarlane, 1995).

Indeed, despite the fact that the overall differences in academic performance are very small, there are still vast differences in the distributions of men and women in different subjects. This can be seen in the percentages of men and women in different disciplines at university (see Table 3).

Subject	% of men	% of women	Total number starting the course
Computer Science	88	12	93
Physics	78	22	37
Philosophy	70	30	71
Music	65	35	34
Earth Sciences	63	37	49
Chemistry	63	37	30
Mathematics	51	49	85
Geography	51	49	132
History	46	54	129
			Continued...

Subject	% of men	% of women	Total number starting the course
Law	43	57	157
Classics	40	60	67
Modern Languages	38	62	170
English	37	63	163
Biology	25	75	57
Sociology	22	78	121
Psychology	21	79	155
Education	15	85	33
Criminology	9	91	93

Note: These figures may vary slightly from year to year, and sample sizes for some groups are small.

Table 3   Percentage of men and women first-year students starting in different subjects at Keele University in 1996

Table 4 shows the percentage of full-time men and women students achieving different degree classes in psychology. The results suggest that men and women now perform equally well at the top end of the distribution, but that men perform worse than women at the bottom end.

Degree class					
Full time	*1st*	*2.1*	*2.2*	*3rd*	Pass
Men (N = 1,234)	6	32	40	3	19
Women (N = 4,513)	6	26	52	1	15

Source: Adapted from figures provided by the Higher Education Statistical Agency, courtesy of the Society for Research in Higher Education

Table 4   Percentage of full-time men and women psychology students achieving different degree classes in 1995

What, then, are psychologists to make of all this? What are the practical implications? By and large the differences between men and women in terms of degree results are small (see Tables 2 and 4) and there is a good deal of overlap — rather like there is in height. Many women students are better than many men students, and vice versa. Both sexes confront difficulties, some of which are common, and some of which are specific. Male nurses, for instance, and women computer scientists may confront different – but sex-related – issues (e.g. see Davidson, 1996; Radford & Holdstock, 1995; Thomas, 1988). But the solution must be for people to try to reduce such obstacles for all learners, and not to regard them as insuperable because of presumed differences between the sexes. And as far as students are concerned – male or female, gay or straight – it is more important for them to develop their own skills of learning in different contexts than it is to worry about sex differences.

Cognitive styles and ways of thinking

Cognitive styles are perhaps less fundamental than are some of the differences listed in Table 1. Reber (1995) defines a cognitive style as 'the characteristic style or manner in which cognitive tasks are approached or handled'. Thus an individual's cognitive style reflects his or her preferred manner of perceiving, remembering and thinking. So, whilst intellectual abilities are primarily concerned with the ability to learn, cognitive styles are primarily concerned with differences in the ways of going about it.

Research suggests that cognitive styles are important variables in two key areas:

1. how students make academic and career choices; and
2. how students learn, how teachers teach, and how these interact.

We shall see both of these issues as we discuss a characteristic example of a cognitive style – that of *convergent* and *divergent* thinking.

Convergent and divergent thinking

In the 1960s there was a growing feeling that typical intelligence tests did not measure all aspects of intelligence. It was argued, for instance, that such tests only measured what was termed 'convergent thinking'. By this it was meant that respondents were required to find a single correct answer to the problem set: their thinking had, as it were, to focus down – or *converge* – on to the one right answer. The opposite of this approach – which, it was argued, was not measured in conventional intelligence tests – was called 'divergent thinking'. This form of thinking is concerned with the capacity to generate responses, to invent new ones, to explore and expand ideas and, in a word, to *diverge*. Convergent thinking thus demands close reasoning; divergent thinking demands fluency and flexibility.

The implications for learning and instruction in this matter centre on three issues: it seems (1) that students who are good at one kind of thinking may not necessarily be good at the other; (2) that students who are good at one kind of thinking may find themselves doing different subjects from students who are good at the other; and (3) that teachers and students may not react well to each other if they do not share the same modes of thinking.

Divergent thinking is usually measured by what are called 'open-ended' tests. Typical items in such tests are *verbal,* such as, 'How many uses can you think of for ...

a brick, a bucket, a paperclip, etc?' or *non-verbal,* such as 'Draw a picture in the space below to illustrate the title "Zebra Crossing"'. Such tests do not require the respondent to produce one right answer – and thus a problem lies in how to score them. Answers are typically scored in terms of:

- Fluency – this measures an individual's ability to produce a large number of ideas in the time allowed. The number of responses given (excluding those that are nonsensical or inappropriate) are scored.

- Flexibility – this measures the ability to produce a wide variety of responses. Responses are grouped into categories and the flexibility score is the number of different categories used.

- Originality – this measures the ability to generate unusual ideas and is based on the most infrequent responses that occur within the group of individuals being tested.

- Elaboration – this measures the ability to develop and expand initial ideas and is based on the amount of detail that the responses contain.

The results from such tests indicate that there are wide individual differences between people on such measures. Box 1 gives some examples from one extreme diverger's answering of a series of different kinds of question reported in a final-year student's psychology project at Keele.

Cognitive styles and academic bias

In 1966, Liam Hudson showed, with 'reasonably clever' fourth-, fifth- and sixth-form boys (i.e. 16–18 year olds), that arts specialists tended to score highly on open-ended divergent thinking tests, whereas science specialists tended to do the reverse, and that this difference was 'massively significant'. These findings followed on from work in the United States, particularly that of Getzels & Jackson (1962). However, because these and other researchers sought – somewhat misleadingly – to equate divergent thinking with creativity and convergent thinking with intelligence, a great deal of controversy ensued. This has continued to the present day (e.g. see Fryer, 1996).

Much of the debate concentrated on the implications of the findings for teaching and learning, and particularly on enhancing creativity at primary and secondary level. None the less, there were some studies that attempted to see how far Hudson's findings about arts and science specialists could be replicated with university students. A recent study in this regard (Hartley & Greggs, 1997) divided students into four groups – those studying arts, those studying arts and social sciences, those studying social sciences and sciences, and those studying science – and all of the students involved completed the four tests listed in Box 1. The results showed that there was weak support for the notion that divergent thinking tests would decline along the arts-science continuum, but that when the four groups were collapsed into two – mostly arts and mostly science – then the arts students did score significantly higher than the science students on all three of the verbal tests, but not significantly so on the visual ('circles') test.

Test 1 Uses of objects

'Listed below are five everyday objects. Think of as many uses as you can for each. You can be as imaginative as you like: a barrel; a paper clip; a tin of boot polish; a brick; a blanket.'

Example responses from a divergent student:
(barrel) put a drink in it; roll it down a hill; squash someone with it; keep stuff in it; take it apart and use it for firewood; try to get into it and make strange noises so that people think there's a ghost around; try to hide a child in it; use it as a toilet; don't use it – keep it as an ornament; throw it away (not scored – inappropriate answer).

Test 2 Word meanings

'Each of the ten words below has more than one meaning. Write down as many meanings as you can for each word: bit, pink, bolt, pitch, duck, port, fair, sack, fast, teacher.'

Example responses from the same divergent student:
(fair) something that's reasonable; someone with easily burnt skin; someone with blonde hair; somewhere you can ride the waltzers at.

Test 3 Common problems

'Write down as many possible problems that might arise when taking a bath.'

Example responses from the same divergent student:
There might be no water; there might be no bath; there might be no hot water; the bath could be too dirty and you don't have any cleaning agents; you might jump in with all your clothes on; it might be too hot when you get in, or too cold; the taps don't work; there's a water shortage in the area and taking a bath is forbidden; you might get soap in your eyes; your next-door neighbour might be making loads of noise and taking a bath means irritation because it's right next to your neighbour; someone else might want a bath at the same time; you might drown; you might get soapy water in your mouth (not scored – a repetition); when you get out you might have forgotten your towel, so you have to run to get one and you're wet and naked; all your towels could be dirty; there's no soap or shampoo left; the bath has a crack in it; you can't get in the bath because you are too fat; you could be real tall and get annoyed when a small portion of you seems able to fit underwater; you might not want a bath; there's no bubble bath (not scored – a repetition).

Continued...

Test 4 Circles test

(Each participant is given a sheet with six rows of five circles drawn on it – all the same size.) 'By using lines, both inside and outside the circles, attempt to make as many different objects as possible. Again you may be as imaginative as you like. If your design is not easily recognisable, you may write a title under each drawing.'

Example responses from the same divergent student:
(All labelled) A bloke, woman, dartboard, spider, brain, beachball, a circular part of Y fronts, face, sun, moon, circle, lollipop, pair of boobs (two circles joined together), balloon, record, odd chair, circular house, someone's foot (not scored – nonsensical), someone's hand (not scored – nonsensical), bird's-eye view of toilet, coin, Scotch video-tape circle, odd-shaped cigarette, a cracked egg, a chick, a dog – woof, woof, bark, a badly drawn lion, a line in a circle (not scored), a square in a circle (not scored).

Box 1   Examples of responses from the same divergent student to four tests used in the study by Hartley & Greggs (1997)

Student-teacher interaction

In general, it seems that members of staff react more favourably to convergent than to divergent students. To put it bluntly, teachers find divergent students difficult to deal with, and this may be especially true of teachers who are themselves convergent thinkers. Such teachers don't like guessing or playfulness, but prefer a 'more serious' approach. If, however, divergent thinking does enhance creative output then teachers need to be made aware of this and persuaded to encourage divergent thinking rather than to respond to such thinking with hostility.

This issue of student-teacher interaction raises the question of whether or not a match or a mismatch in cognitive style makes for better learning.

Witkin (1976) proposed that individuals matched in cognitive style were likely to get along better because they would have:

- Shared foci of interest – individuals with the same cognitive style have a shared tendency to attend to the same aspects of the environment.

- Shared personal characteristics – individuals matched in cognitive style are likely to share similar views, dress in a similar manner and so on.

- Similar modes of communication – individuals with the same cognitive style tend to be on the same 'wavelength' and, for example, use similar non-verbal gestures to accompany speech.

Whether or not a match in cognitive style between student and teacher makes for better student learning is uncertain, as research in this area has produced mixed results. One might argue that a mismatch in cognitive style, providing it is not too great, can benefit student learning. In the case of cognitive styles where a greater value is placed on one end of the dimension than on the other, a teacher with a slightly more positive style than the student may encourage the student to develop in this respect (Hayes & Allinson, 1996).

It is, of course, difficult to carry out studies to assess the effects of matching and mismatching teachers and students on any particular measure. Some such studies have, however, been carried out in the United States, where student class sizes are generally much larger than in the United Kingdom (see, for example, Domino, 1971). However, with the advent of computer-assisted learning ... we may expect an increase in the number of studies that try to match learning styles to methods of instruction. The following papers illustrate the beginnings of this approach: Kwok & Jones (1995); Liu & Reed (1994); and Paterson & Rosbottom (1995).

Learning strategies

The strategies that learners use to learn and study are – sometimes – more consciously initiated and controlled than are their learning styles. Learning strategies are thought to be less general and less fixed. Different strategies are selected by learners to deal with different tasks.

Deep and surface learning One learning strategy currently receiving much attention is whether or not students adopt a 'deep' or a 'surface' approach to studying. Here the story begins in the 1970s. In a series of studies conducted in Sweden, Ferenc Marton and his colleagues asked students how they studied written texts. The replies of the students were categorised either as those of 'deep' or those of 'surface' processors. Deep processors gave replies like: 'I try to get at the principal ideas'; 'I try to find the main points of the chapter'; 'I think about how the author has built up his argument.' Surface processors give replies like: 'I just read straight through from start to finish'; 'I try to concentrate on remembering as much as possible'; 'I didn't remember what I read because I was thinking of hurrying on'. Deep processors, it appears, try to extract meaning from the text: surface processors concentrate on remembering the text itself.

Research has shown that the method of processing that students use has a marked effect upon how well they learn. In one study, Marton & Saljo (1976) asked students to read a 1,400-word article on the topic of curriculum reform in Swedish universities. In the article itself the author had argued that a sweeping reform, aimed at raising university pass rates uniformly, was misguided because different groups of students had different pass rates. The author suggested, therefore, that selective measures should be taken that would concentrate on those particular classes of students that had low pass rates.

After reading the article, the students were asked, 'Try to summarise the article in one or two sentences. What is the author trying to say, in other words?' It was found that the responses could be classified in four ways:

1. Those that reported that there were differences in the pass rates between groups of students.

2. Those that reported that measures were to be taken.

3. Those that reported that different measures should be taken with different groups of students.

4. Those that reported that selective measures should be taken, i.e. only for particular categories of students with low pass rates.

... When these replies were analysed with reference to whether or not the students were considered to be deep or surface learners... [it was clear that] the students' approaches to reading the text had had a marked effect. None of the students labelled 'surface' processors had adequately summarised the main points of the article, whereas none of the students labelled 'deep' processors had failed to do so...

Findings, such as [these] were replicated in many countries (see Ramsden, 1992). However, more important, some of these studies also showed that students varied their reading strategies (e.g. Laurillard, 1979). Thus the same student might be a surface processor in some conditions and a deep processor in others, depending upon the nature of the task. Such learners were labelled 'strategic'.

In the 1990s, the research began to turn to trying to ascertain what factors might help students to be deep rather than surface processors. Gibbs (1992: 9) outlined some of the conditions that encourage *surface* processing as follows:

- a heavy workload
- relatively high class contact hours
- an excessive amount of course material
- a lack of opportunity to pursue subjects in depth
- a lack of choice over subjects, and a lack of choice over the methods of study
- a threatening and anxiety-provoking assessment system.

Some of the teaching strategies that encourage *deep* processing include:

- project work
- learning by doing
- using problem-based learning
- setting assignments that cannot be completed by memory work alone
- using group assignments
- encouraging student reflection
- allowing for independent learning
- providing authentic tasks
- rewarding understanding and penalising reproduction
- involving students in the choice of assessment methods...

Preferences

Preferences are less fixed than learning strategies. They may be deep seated but not of major concern to a particular learner. Here I take seating preferences as my example.

Seating preferences

Most studies of seating preferences, and the effects of different seating arrangements on learning, have taken place in primary and secondary schools rather than in universities. None the less, the findings appear to have some relevance to the latter situation. These findings generally suggest that more discussion takes place if pupils are seated around tables than seated in rows, and that more 'on-task' behaviour occurs when pupils are seated in rows rather than around tables (Hastings *et al.* 1996).

Figure 1, opposite, shows a variety of different seating patterns. Feitler and colleagues (1971) reported what happened when university students and teachers were asked to decide which teaching arrangements they would find most comfortable, and which least. The results showed that both students and teachers said that they would feel most comfortable in setting seven. Many of them also picked settings five and two.

Settings one and six were chosen by both teachers and students as being the least comfortable. Despite the general popularity of settings two and seven, many thought that these settings would be uncomfortable for students. The researchers were surprised by the choice of setting six as the least comfortable. It was surprising, they said, because 'the concept of students working in small groups with the teacher helping as needed would appear as one which is desirable and often used, particularly in science laboratory work'. It may be, however, that this result arose from the fact that the schematic diagram did not make clear the flexible role of the teacher (compared with setting two, which was liked by many).

Other studies of seating preferences have suggested that when communication is free:

- the maximum number of communications is made between people sitting opposite each other;
- the minimum number of communications is made by people sitting next to each other;
- the most centrally placed person is likely to emerge as the group leader; and
- leaders are most likely to emerge on that side of the table that has the fewest people.

Other studies with schoolchildren seated in rows have suggested that children receive more or less questions from their teachers as a function of the rows in which they are seated (see Hastings *et al.* 1996). Thus children at the front of a room may receive more questions than those seated at the back.

In a lecture setting, of course, most students choose where they want to sit. None the less there is often some consistency in their choice. In the United States there have been several studies of students' seating preferences, and how they relate to examination results or changes in achievement motivation. According to Burda & Brooks (1996), the evidence suggests that as students sit further back, their attention

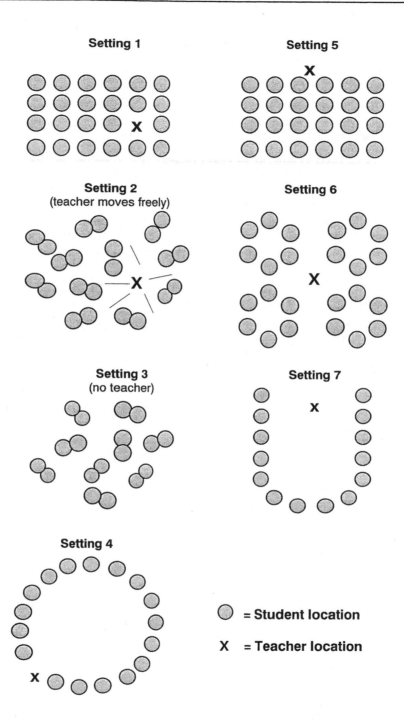

Figure 1 Some possible seating arrangements
(Diagram printed with permission from Psychology Today magazine,
copyright © 1971, Sussex Publishers, Inc.)

and participation decreases, their attendance decreases, and their academic grades decline. Burda & Brooks also note that students who sit near the front have more positive attitudes to learning, and have higher self-esteem and less anxiety. Of course, this does not mean that everyone should sit in the front row(!) but it might suggest that students can improve their grades by sitting nearer the front. (Brooks & Rebeta, 1991, note that more women than men sit in the front rows.) The crucial question in all of these studies, of course, is do good students choose to sit at the front, or does sitting at the front lead to better grades?...

Finally, we should note here that the effects of seating position may be confounded with that of the size of the class. Currently, lecture-group sizes are increasing in the UK, and an issue that is now of key concern is that of the effects of increasing class size on learning. Students interested in pursuing this debate might like to read the reviews by McKeachie (1994) and Gibbs *et al.* (1996) on the effects of class size on learning, and also the study by Perera & Hartley (1997) on the effects of crowding on learning.

Concluding remarks

To conclude this chapter it might be appropriate to comment on the methods that psychologists have used to study individual differences in learning. We have seen that a variety of methods have been used: interviews, questionnaires, qualitative and quantitative studies. Some studies have been quite simple – participants have completed questionnaires and total scores have been correlated with some measure of academic achievement. Or groups have been subdivided on some scale (e.g. of convergence/divergence) and the performance of groups at each end of the scale has been compared, sometimes in different conditions using *analysis of variance*.

More complex studies have administered several questionnaires and tried to work out – using *multiple regression* techniques – which factors are most important in determining success. Wolfe & Johnson (1995), for instance, pooled measures of academic success with those from thirty-two personality variables in trying to predict the academic performance of a group of American psychology students. They found that previous academic success and scores on a measure of locus of control were the most important measures.

Other investigators have administered several questionnaires and then used *cluster analysis* to find different 'clusters', or groups of respondents that are similar in some ways but different from other groups (e.g. Entwistle & Brennan, 1971). The advent of computer-based testing, scoring and analysing results may lead to an increase in these kinds of studies.

Finally, many investigators have carried out – or reported – meta-analyses (e.g. Halpern, 1992). Today, these rather mechanical – and quantitative – approaches are being supplemented, and indeed sometimes replaced, by more qualitative ones. In studying the academic performance of older students, for instance, there is now a greater willingness to consider case histories and interview data.

References

Abouserie R (1995) 'Self-esteem and achievement motivation as determinants of students' approaches to studying' *Studies in Higher Education* 20 (1), pp19–26

Archer J (1996) 'Sex differences in social behaviour: are the social role and evolutionary explanations compatible?' *American Psychologist* 51 (9), pp909–917

Brooks CI & Rebeta JL (1991) 'College classroom ecology: the relation of sex to classroom performance and seating preference' *Environment and Behavior* 23 (3), pp305–313

Burda JM & Brooks CI (1996) 'College classroom seating position and changes in achievement motivation over a semester' *Psychological Reports* 78, pp331–336

Chalmers D & Fuller R (1996) *Teaching for learning at university* Kogan Page

Clarke S (1988) 'Another look at the degree results of men and women' *Studies in Higher Education* 13 (3), pp315–331

Davidson MJ (1996) 'Women and employment' in PB Warr (ed) *Psychology at work* 4th edn Penguin Books

Davies B & Harré R (1989) 'Introduction to special issue: gender, education and current issues' *Oxford Review of Education* 15 (3), pp213–214

Domino G (1971) 'Interactive effects of achievement orientation and teaching style on academic achievement' *Journal of Educational Psychology* 62, pp427–431

Entwistle NJ & Brennan T (1971) 'The academic performance of students: 2. Types of successful students' *British Journal of Educational Psychology* 41 (3), pp268–276

Eysenck HJ & Eysenck MW (1985) *Personality and individual differences: a natural science approach* Plenum

Feitler FC *et al.* (1971) Study reported in *Psychology Today* September, p12

Fryer M (1996) *Creative teaching and learning* Paul Chapman

Getzels JW & Jackson PW (1962) *Creativity and intelligence: explorations with gifted students* Wiley

Gibbs G (ed) (1992) *Improving the quality of student learning* Technical and Educational Services Ltd

Gibbs G, Lucas L & Simonite V (1996) 'Class size and student performance: 1984–94' *Studies in Higher Education* 21 (3), pp261–274

Goldman BA & Flake WL (1996) 'Is flexibility related to college achievement? A five-year study' *Psychological Reports* 78, pp337–338

Greenwood KM (1995) 'An evaluation of the circadian type questionnaire' *Ergonomics* 38 (2), pp347–360

Halpern DE (1992) *Sex differences in cognitive abilities* 2nd edn Erlbaum

Hartley J & Greggs MA (1997) 'Divergent thinking in arts and science students: *Contrary Imaginations* at Keele revisited' *Studies in Higher Education* 22 (1), pp93–97

Hastings N, Schweiso J & Wheldhall K (1996) 'A place for learning' in P Croll & N Hastings (eds) *Effective primary teaching* David Fulton

Hayes J & Allinson C (1996) 'The implications of learning styles for training and development: a discussion of the matching hypothesis' *British Journal of Management* 7, pp63–73

Hayes K & Richardson JTE (1995) 'Gender, subject and context as determinants of approaches to studying in higher education' *Studies in Higher Education* 20 (2), pp215–221

Hudson L (1966) *Contrary imaginations* Methuen

Jonassen DH & Grabowski BL (1993) *Handbook of individual differences, learning, and instruction* Erlbaum

Kirby JR (1993) 'Collaborative and competitive effects of verbal and spatial processes' *Learning and Instruction* 3, pp201–214

Kwok M & Jones C (1995) 'Catering for different learning styles' *ALT Journal* 3 (1), pp5–11

Laurillard D (1979) 'The process of student learning' *Higher Education* 8 (4), pp395–410

Liu M & Reed WM (1994) 'The relationship between the learning strategies and learning styles in a hypermedia environment' *Computers in Human Behavior* 10 (4), pp419–434

Maccoby EE & Jacklin CN (1974) *The psychology of sex differences* Oxford University Press

McKeachie WJ (1994) *Teaching tips: strategies, research, and theory for college and university teachers* 9th edn Heath

McNamara D & Harris R (eds) (1997) *Overseas students in higher education: issues in teaching and learning* Routledge

Marton F & Saljo R (1976) 'On qualitative differences in student learning: 1. outcome and process' *British Journal of Educational Psychology* 46 (1), pp4–11

Millar R & Irving P (1995) 'Academic locus of control in British undergraduate students' *British Journal of Educational Psychology* 65 (3), pp331–340

Paterson P & Rosbottom J (1995) 'Learning style and learning strategies in a multimedia environment' *ALT Journal* 3 (1), pp12–21

Perera D & Hartley J (1997) 'The costs of crowded classrooms' *New Academic* 6 (2), pp17–18

Radford J & Holdstock L (1995) 'Gender differences in higher education aims between Computing and Psychology students' *Research in Science and Technological Education* 13 (2), pp163–176

Ramsden P (1992) *Learning to teach in higher education* Routledge

Reber AS (1995) *The Penguin dictionary of psychology* Penguin

Riding RJ & Rayner SG (eds) (1997) 'Learning styles and strategies' *Educational Psychology* 17 (1/2), pp5–225

Rudd E (1984) 'A comparison between the results achieved by women and men studying for first degrees in British education' *Studies in Higher Education* 9 (1), pp47–57

Rudd E (1988) 'Reply to Clarke' *Studies in Higher Education* 13 (3), pp333–336

Sadler-Smith E (1996) 'Approaches to studying: age, gender and academic performance' *Educational Studies* 22 (3), pp367–379

Santostefano S (1985) *Cognitive control therapy with children and adolescents* Pergamon

Sutherland P (ed) (1997) *Adult learning: a reader* Kogan Page

Thomas K (1988) 'Gender and the arts/science divide in higher education' *Studies in Higher Education* 13 (2), pp123–137

Tobias S (1994) 'Interest, prior knowledge and learning' *Review of Educational Research* 64 (1), pp37–54

Tomlinson K & Macfarlane B (1995) 'The significance of subject choice in explaining the first-class degree divide between male and female graduates' *Research in Education* 54, pp95–100

Willcoxson L & Prosser M (1996) 'Kolb's learning style inventory (1985): review and further study of validity and reliability' *British Journal of Educational Psychology* 66 (2), pp247–258

Witkin H (1976) 'Cognitive style in academic performance and in teacher-student relations' in S Messick and associates *Individuality in learning* Jossey Bass

Wolfe RN & Johnson SD (1995) 'Personality as a predictor of college performance' *Educational and Psychological Measurement* 55 (2), pp177–185

Wong CT, Day JJ, Maxwell SE & Meara NM (1995) 'A multitrait-multimethod study of academic and social intelligence in college students' *Journal of Educational Psychology* 87 (1), pp117–133

Zeidner M (1996) 'How do high school and college students cope with test situations' *British Journal of Educational Psychology* 66 (1), pp115–128

Further reading

Baxter Magolda MB (1992) *Knowing and reasoning: patterns in students' intellectual development* Jossey Bass. This text looks at differences between men and women students in terms of how they think and reason.

Eysenck HJ (1995) *Genius: the natural history of creativity* Cambridge University Press. A useful review of psychological research in this area.

5.   Cultural Diversity

Ann Lahiff

This section examines some of the key educational concepts with regard to individual differences and diversity from the perspective of the discipline of sociology. It will offer the opportunity to explore the 'sociological approach' and reflect upon how such an exploration might inform an understanding of some of the factors affecting learning.

Much of the approach is set within the context of discussions that derive from the sociology of education of the last 20 years. As will be seen, some of the issues remain the same, despite the passage of time. Others are unique to education and training in Britain as we move into the 21st century.

I begin by setting out the nature of sociological inquiry, distinguishing the approach from that provided by psychology. This is followed by an outline of a key concept – culture – and leads to an appreciation of what is meant by the notion of 'cultural diversity'.

The sociological approach

We need to distinguish how a sociological approach differs from a psychological approach. To help us do this it is useful to establish some of the things they have in common. Both are, for example, concerned with understanding *social* phenomena and they form part of the social sciences. In some respects they form a continuum of explanation, overlapping in the area of social psychology.

In terms of distinguishing the approaches, it can be said that sociology is concerned with understanding how people operate in groups: family groups, religious groups, peer groups, students, teachers, ethnic groups, etc. Sociologists want to understand such things as why the groups take the form they do, how they interact, who is running them and how they are perceived by others.

Most sociologists are concerned with the wider context too, offering explanations of the inter-relationships between parts of a whole society. Whilst psychologists may concern themselves with the *individual*, the sociologist is largely concerned with the individual only in so far as s/he connects with others. For example, unlike (some) psychologists, they show less concern with what is going on in the individual's mind or their personality type. Instead, sociologists would be more interested in how individual differences are patterned and shaped by the way that our societies are organised.

Sociology, then – distinguishable by its distinctive assumptions, concepts and questions – presents an approach to the study of social life.

Anthony Giddens chooses a couple of surprising examples of this.

What is sociology about? Some examples

Love and marriage

Why do people fall in love and get married? The answer at first sight seems obvious. Love expresses a mutual physical and personal attachment which two individuals feel for one another. These days, many of us might be sceptical of the idea that love 'is for ever', but 'falling in love', we tend to think, derives from universal human sentiments and emotions. It seems entirely natural for a couple who fall in love to want to set up house together, and to seek personal and sexual fulfilment in their relationship.

Yet this view, which seems so self-evident, is in fact quite unusual. Falling in love is not an experience most human beings have, and it is rarely associated with marriage. The idea of romantic love did not become widespread until fairly recently in the West, and has never existed in most other cultures. It is only in modern times that love, marriage and sexuality have been regarded as closely bound up with one another. In the Middle Ages, and for centuries afterwards, people married mainly in order to perpetuate the ownership of a title or property in the hands of family, or to raise children to work the family farm.

Once married, they may sometimes have become close companions; this happened after marriage, however, rather than before. There were sexual liaisons outside marriage, but these involved few of the sentiments we connect with love. Love was regarded 'as at best a necessary weakness and at worst a kind of sickness' (Monter, 1977: 123).

Romantic love first made its appearance in courtly circles, as a characteristic of extra-marital sexual adventures indulged in by members of the aristocracy. Until about two centuries ago, it was wholly confined to such circles, and kept specifically separated from marriage. Relations between husband and wife among aristocratic groups were often cool and distant – certainly compared to our expectations of marriage today. The wealthy lived in large houses, each spouse having his or her own bedroom and servants; they may rarely have seen each other in private. Sexual compatibility was a matter of hazard, and was not considered relevant to marriage. Among both rich and poor, the decision to marry was taken by family and kin, not by the individuals concerned, who had little or no say in the matter. (This remains true in many non-western cultures in current times.)

Neither romantic love then, nor its association with marriage, can be understood as 'given' features of human life, but are shaped by broad social influences. These are the influences sociologists study – and which make themselves felt even in seemingly purely personal experiences. Most of us see the world in terms of familiar features of our own lives. Sociology demonstrates the need to take a much wider view of why we act as we do.

Health and illness

We normally think of health and illness as matters concerned only with the physical condition of the body. A person feels aches and pains, or gets feverish. How could

Continued...

this have anything to do with wider influences of a social kind? In fact, social factors have a profound effect upon both the experience and the occurrence of illness, as well as upon how we react to being ill. Our very concept of 'illness', as involving physical malfunctioning of the body, is not shared by people in all societies. Sickness, and even death, are thought of in some other cultures as produced by evil spells, not by treatable physical causes (Evans-Pritchard, 1950). In our society, Christian Scientists reject much orthodox thinking about illness, believing that we are really spiritual and perfect in the image of God, sickness coming from a misunderstanding of reality, 'letting error in'.

How long one can expect to live, and the chances of contracting serious diseases such as heart troubles, cancer or pneumonia, are all strongly influenced by social characteristics. The more affluent the background people are from, the less likely they will be to suffer from a serious illness at any point in their lives. In addition, there are strongly defined social rules about how we are expected to behave when we become ill. A person who is ill is excused from many or all of the normal duties of everyday life, but the sickness has to be acknowledged as 'serious enough' to be able to claim these benefits without criticism or rebuke. Someone who is thought to be suffering only from a relatively mild form of infirmity, or whose illness has not been precisely identified, is likely to be seen as a 'malingerer' – as not really having the right to escape from daily obligations (Segal, 1976; Cockerham, 1986)...

Implications: the nature of sociology

At this point we can take stock of the examples discussed so far. In each of the cases – love, marriage and sexuality, and health and illness – we have seen that what might be seen to be 'naturally given' human sentiments and feelings are in fact pervasively influenced by social factors. An understanding of the subtle, yet complex and profound, ways in which our lives reflect the contexts of our social experience is basic to the sociological outlook. Sociology focuses in particular upon social life in the *modern world* – the world brought into being by the sweeping changes in human societies which have occurred over the past two centuries or so.

References

Cockerham WC (1986) *Medical sociology* 3rd edn Prentice-Hall
Evans-Pritchard E (1950) *Witchcraft, oracles and magic among the Azande* Oxford University Press
Monter E (1977) 'The pedestal and the stake: courtly love and witchcraft' in R Bridenthal & C Koonz *Becoming visible: women in European history* Houghton, Mifflin
Segal A (1976) 'The sick role concept: understanding illness behaviour' *Journal of Health and Social Behaviour* 17

(Giddens, 1989: 8–11)

In the next short reading Ian Marsh presents a wide definition of the business of sociology, emphasising the role of the human being as a 'social animal' set in a public context, extending experience beyond the merely personal while encompassing aspects of biography and history.

Making sense of society

In the writings of Berger (1967) and CW Mills (1970), and more recent contributions from Bauman (1990) and Kingdom (1991), we get a very strong notion of what sociology is, often as a result of stressing what it is not. They make clear that sociology is an antidote to personal and subjective observations and a complete rejection of explanations that are grounded in naturalistic or individualistic assumptions about 'human nature'. The emphasis is quite clearly upon the individual as a social animal within the context of a social environment. As this emphasis challenges popular and sometimes deeply held notions of human nature and individual responsibility it is not surprising that sociology meets with a certain amount of resistance. Anticipating what has become known as the 'structure versus agency debate', CW Mills pointed out in his introduction to *The Sociological Imagination* (1970) that the primary role of the sociologist is to reveal the complex relationship between the individual and society:

The sociological imagination enables us to grasp history and biography and the relations between the two within society. That is its task and its promise. To recognise this task and this promise is the mark of the classic social analyst... No social study that does not come back to the problem of biography, of history, and of their intersections within a society, has completed its intellectual journey.

(Mills, 1970: 12)

Mills demonstrates that by unifying biography and history we are forced to place our own individual experiences and attitudes in the context of social structure and that societies themselves are not unique but have to be placed within an historical context.

Thus we have to go beyond personal experience and common sense for answers to our questions. The most vivid example can be seen in Mills's distinction between 'personal troubles' and 'public issues'. Whether we are looking at unemployment, war, divorce or the problems of urban living, there are aspects of our lives over which we have some control – 'personal troubles' for which we bear some responsibility and to which we can offer some private solution. However, there are other conditions that offer no such remedy because the troubles that we experience (no matter how personally) are beyond our control; they have historical and structural causes and as such represent 'public issues' which can be changed only by large-scale economic developments or social reform.

Writing twenty years later Zygmunt Bauman reiterates the importance of Mills's early insights into the crucial relationship between history, society and biography:

Deeply immersed in our daily routines, though, we hardly ever pause to think about the meaning of what we have gone through: even less often have we the opportunity to compare our private experience with the fate of others; to see the social in the individual, the general in the particular, this is precisely what sociologists can do for us. We would expect them to show us how our individual biographies intervene with the history we share with fellow human beings.

(Bauman, 1990; quoted in Giddens, 1992: 8)

Continued...

References

Bauman Z (1990) *Thinking sociologically* Blackwell

Berger PL (1967) *Invitation to sociology: a humanistic perspective* Penguin

Giddens A (ed) (1992) *Human societies: an introductory reader in sociology* Polity Press

Kingdom J (1991) *Government and politics in Britain* Polity Press

Mills CW (1970) *The sociological imagination* Penguin

(Marsh *et al.* 1996: 7)

Each of these extracts emphasises the task of the sociologist as one of understanding the relationship between the individual and society, the relationship between the private sphere and the public sphere. Developing an appreciation of this relationship is crucial in any consideration of the factors affecting learning as a social activity in the PCET environment.

In the next contribution Giddens gives a vivid demonstration of the role that the sociologist has to play in 'making the familiar strange'.

Cultural identity and ethnocentrism

Every culture contains its own unique patterns of behaviour, which seem alien to people from other cultural backgrounds. As an example, we can take the Nacirema, a group described in a celebrated research investigation by Horace Miner (1956). Miner concentrated his attention on the elaborate body-rituals in which the Nacirema engage, rituals which have strange and exotic characteristics. His discussion is worth quoting at length:

The fundamental belief underlying the whole system appears to be that the human body is ugly and that its natural tendency is to debility and disease. Incarcerated in such a body, man's [sic] only hope is to avert these characteristics through the use of the powerful influences of ritual and ceremony. Every household has one or more shrines devoted to this purpose... The focal point of the shrine is a box or chest which is built into the wall. In this chest are kept the many charms and magical potions without which no native believes he could live. These preparations are secured from a variety of specialized practitioners. The most powerful of these are the medicine men, whose assistance must be rewarded with substantial gifts. However, the medicine men do not provide the curative potions for their clients, but decide what the ingredients should be and then write them down in an ancient and secret language. This writing is understood only by the medicine men and by the herbalists who, for another gift, provide the required charm...

The Nacirema have an almost pathological horror of and fascination with the mouth, the condition of which is believed to have a supernatural influence on all social relationships. Were it not for the rituals of the mouth, they believe that their teeth would fall out, their gums bleed, their jaws shrink, their friends desert them,

Continued...

and their lovers reject them. They also believe that a strong relationship exists between oral and moral characteristics. For example, there is a ritual ablution of the mouth for children which is supposed to improve their moral fibre.

The daily body ritual performed by everyone includes a mouth-rite. Despite the fact that these people are so punctilious about care of the mouth, this rite involves a practice which strikes the uninitiated stranger as revolting. It was reported to me that the ritual consists of inserting a small bundle of hog hairs into the mouth, along with certain magical powders, and then moving the bundle in a highly formalized series of gestures.

(Miner, 1956)

Reference

Miner H (1956) 'Body ritual among the Nacirema' *American Anthropologist* 58

(Giddens, 1997: 23–24)

'The way we do things round here' is perhaps one of the more accessible definitions of what we mean by 'culture'. Giddens explains it in terms of norms, values, language and conventions.

The concept of culture

The concepts of culture and society ... are among the most widely used notions in sociology. When we use the word 'culture' in ordinary daily conversation, we often think of 'culture' as equivalent to the 'higher things of the mind' – art, literature, music and painting. As sociologists use the term, it includes such activities, but also far more. Culture refers to the ways of life of the members of a society, or of groups within a society. It includes how they dress, their marriage customs and family life, their patterns of work, religious ceremonies and leisure pursuits.

'Culture' can be conceptually distinguished from 'society', but there are very close connections between these notions. A society is a *system of interrelationships* which connects individuals together. Britain, France and the United States are societies in this sense. They include millions of people; ... some societies are very much smaller.

No cultures could exist without societies. But, equally, no societies could exist without culture. Without culture, we would not be 'human' at all, in the sense in which we usually understand that term. We would have no language in which to express ourselves, no sense of self-consciousness, and our ability to think or reason would be severely limited. How far do characteristics like these distinguish human beings from the animals? Where do our distinctively 'human' characteristics come from? What is the nature of human nature? These questions are crucial to sociology, because they set the foundation for the whole field of study. To answer them, we [need to] analyse both what as human beings we share and how we differ.

(Giddens, 1997: 18)

Culture then, is a *social creation* – whether it is seen as 'out there' waiting to be learned by new members of society or 'in here' in the consciousness of members of society – being created by them in their everyday lives. Our behaviour, our attitudes and our values are guided by the cultural framework in which we live.

Of course many of us operate in a number of contexts and are influenced by a range of 'communities' – whether they be families, religious groups or political organisations, as well as social classes and ethnic groups. Indeed, some would argue that whenever a group of people interact in a given context, they create a culture or *sub-culture* which may be temporary or more long-lasting. This gives rise to the recognition that we may embrace (and probably do) more than one culture, as Patrick McNeill recognises in his exploration of language as a cultural artefact.

Language and culture

The use of language is one of the most important ways in which human beings differ from other animals. Most animal species can, of course, communicate with each other, and some can transmit quite complex messages. But when an animal communicates with its fellows, it selects a signal or signals from a finite range available to it. What a human being can do, and we are unique in this, is to assemble a group of signals (words) in a way that no one has ever done before, transmit them, and, provided that we observe basic rules, make ourselves understood. We can say things that no one has ever said before, and be understood.

Furthermore, human language can deal in abstractions, and so discussion can take place. Human beings can discuss possibilities, and can reflect on and choose between alternative views or courses of action. We can make plans. It is this ability to reflect, to be consciously aware of ourselves and our relationship with our environment, that distinguishes human beings from other animals. And it is language that is the key to this ability.

... Social interaction is only possible between people who share some cultural background, however limited. Their interaction is conducted through a shared language. If they have no words in common, they can interact to a limited degree by interpreting each other's gestures. But they cannot get beyond the basic level until they share language. Culture is the basis of social interaction, and language is the vehicle of culture. The study of language is therefore fundamentally important in the study of human social behaviour.

To be a member of a group or society is to share in its culture, and thus to see the world as other group-members do. We feel at ease with those who, broadly speaking, share our world-view. You may have heard or used the everyday expression, 'Yes, I like him – he speaks my language.' This does not mean, literally, that he speaks English, but that he thinks as I do, responds as I do, and shares my assumptions. Language, therefore, binds a group together. This is especially obvious in the case of some subcultural groups, whose private slang and vocabulary enable them to identify each other and to exclude others, especially authority, from the group.

Continued...

This great importance of language has been increasingly recognised by philosophers and sociologists during this century. Phenomenologists, particularly, have given language a central role in their theory of social life... Their basic theme is that the individual socially constructs his or her reality, and they regard society as an immensely elaborate construct of shared meanings, continually created and recreated in interaction.

Since language is the tool used to create and sustain this shared reality, reality to an extent depends on and exists in language. Indeed, what is 'really' so may be changeable by using different words to refer to it. If we think of 'old age pensioners' as 'senior citizens', does this change our attitude to them, and their own self-image? If it does change our attitude, then our behaviour towards them will change. In that case, they will *really* be a different phenomenon from that which they were originally. By referring to someone as a 'terrorist' or as a 'freedom-fighter', we are not only making our attitude clear, but also implying what action should be taken towards them. Whether we refer to the 'foetus' or the 'unborn child' has crucial implications for our views on the morality of 'terminating' it, or 'killing' it...

Language, then, gives meaning to our experience by organizing it. When a young child first sees a furry four-legged animal with a tail, his [sic] parent may say 'dog', and the child will learn the word, and hence share the experience. Then next time he sees a furry quadruped with a tail, he may say 'dog' and be told 'No – cat'. After a number of similar experiences, the child learns that animals as varied as a chihuahua and an alsatian are all dogs, and that cats, some of which may look very similar in appearance to some dogs, are a separate species – or, rather, that they are defined as a separate species in our culture. The child learns too that, whereas Mummy is a woman, not all women are Mummies, and still less are they all his Mummy. But it is only through his use of the word 'Mummy' that he can learn that, to the little girl next door, another woman is Mummy. He can learn that her relationship to her Mummy is of the same order as his relationship to his Mummy. He can thus learn to abstract the concept of Mummy from his experience, and apply it in other contexts.

Language also enables us to share experiences which we have not had first-hand. I have never seen an angry African elephant charging through the undergrowth at me, but I have read accounts of it in books. I thus have some idea of what it is like, I have an attitude towards it as an experience, and I think I know how I would react. Indeed we know most of what we know only because others have told us about it, in language. Most of our experience, and hence our knowledge, is second-hand and is filtered to us by others, through language...

Language, then, enables us to make sense of and share our experience. But how far does it limit our experience, by organizing it in one particular way to the exclusion of others? Initially, language may be thought of simply as labels applied to an objective 'out-there' reality. But, if language is understood as giving meaning to reality, it follows that a different language may give a different meaning to experience. Experience, and so reality, may vary according to which language is used to give it meaning.

Continued...

72

The question is: can we experience something for which we have no word? Or, more sociologically, can we share an experience with others if we cannot express it in language?

The philosopher Wittgenstein maintained that the world in English is different from the world in French, that is, that English speakers actually perceive a different reality from French-speakers. [Basil] Bernstein has argued that children whose language-code is different from that used in schools may under-achieve because their use of language and thus their perception of experience is different from that of their teachers. According to Wittgenstein (1921), 'The limits of my language are the limits of my world', that is, I cannot give meaning to that which I cannot express in language. If I cannot give it meaning, I cannot organize it into my experience or share it with others. If I cannot do this, it is, in a very basic sense, not real to me.

The Eskimo has over twenty different words for snow. Does this mean that snow for the Eskimo is a different and more complex phenomenon than it is for you and me? If it is different, can I ever wholly share in the Eskimo experience of snow?

Language, then, is both essential for us to interpret our experience and to become social, and at the same time it limits what we are able to experience. It is, therefore, a social institution like any other, created by human beings and yet exercising control over us, regulating our patterns of thought and our relations with others, making many things possible and many others impossible.

Reference

Wittgenstein L (1921) *Tractatus logico-philosophicus* Routledge & Kegan Paul

(McNeill, 1981: 116–118)

As McNeill suggests, language is often a defining feature of culture. Whilst there are different symbolic systems which represent the social and natural world, the question of whether there is a 'natural' superiority of one over the other has dogged the world of linguistics. Most would agree that each had its own rationale and legitimacy, neither being more intrinsically valid or relevant than the other. However, once one system of representation (one language) is used by 'the teacher', to the exclusion or side-lining of another, status and value is given or ascribed. It becomes the language all must use – any other becomes secondary. We should also remember that language conveys implicit messages besides the explicit one: i.e. messages about your values and/or the values of wider society. For instance, using the term 'foreigner' to describe people from different ethnic minority groups irrespective of their personal history conveys the view that they do not belong. Similarly, describing a particular social world as being full of *men,* living together as *mankind* with enough *manpower* to keep the institution *manned* does much to contribute to the subordination of women in a society dominated by men.

Debates raged in the 70s and early 80s in relation to use of 'Standard English' and 'Non-Standard English' and was primarily concerned with this debate about

73

superiority. Basil Bernstein's work on so-called 'elaborated' and 'restricted' codes is perhaps the most well known. It is certainly the most discussed! But it is now reasonably safe to say that the debates have moved on from suggestions that some language forms are deficient in relation to others. Most educationalists today would agree that languages can be seen to have their own structures, syntax, grammar without one being intrinsically superior to another.

The arguments about deficiency are therefore not played out in quite the same way as they were in 70s and 80s, but the ability to use different language types is still an issue. There is no doubt that there is a greater continuity of culture between the educational environment and the home for some groups of learners than for others (and this is particularly the case for language use). For those students whose language use at home is closer to that used in the educational environment, there will be less of a hurdle to jump in the learning process. But for others, what will their experience be and how will it effect learning?

Different but not deficient

The diversity of human culture is considerable and, following on from the understanding of culture presented above, it would be a mistake to suppose that just because colleagues or students dressed alike, had the same first language as you, and had an appearance similar to your own, that they shared the same cultural world. As will be seen, often the *assumptions* that we make about learners are crucial in determining our relationships with them and, ultimately, their success or otherwise.

So, one central point to make is that *different* does not mean *deficient*. Identifying a 'clash of cultures' has led many to suggest that this explains the differences in achievement/outcomes of many groups in compulsory and post-compulsory education.

In the next section, on *Access and Opportunity*, you will note how often 'explanations' of differences in educational outcomes rest on the recognition of differences in cultures.

Self-fulfilling prophecy and labelling theory

An area of theory that has been used extensively by educationalists to explain the diversity of student experiences in education has been 'labelling' theory and the significance of the 'self-fulfilling prophecy'. Providing a short account of these now will enable you to consider how these theories might be used in the sections that follow.

Imagine a situation where you are about to take responsibility for a group of students or trainees. You've not met them before, but as you prepare to go into the group a colleague says to you, 'I pity you taking them – they are quite a mixed bunch. Amy and Clare are really dull, but Shaun and Jayesh are bright enough...' and then wanders off.

The *self-fulfilling prophecy* theory would suggest that once your colleague defined named students as bright or dull, you would make predictions and prophecies about their behaviour and/or aptitude. Interaction would be shaped by the definition of the student – expecting little of the 'dull' student and much of the 'bright' student. Expectations are conveyed by the teacher/trainer's manner, facial expression, feedback and so on. The crucial point about the notion of the self-fulfilling prophecy is that the student's *self-concept* will, in all likelihood, be shaped by the teacher/trainer's definition – seeing him/herself as bright or dull. In these ways the prophecy is fulfilled: the predictions made by the teacher/trainer have been realised.

With a self-fulfilling prophecy, it is the *public definitions* of the situation (the prophecies or predictions) which become an integral part of the situation and thus affect subsequent developments.

Like the self-fulfilling prophecy, *labelling theory* has been used to explain some of the effects on students that a teacher/trainer's definitions may have. Labelling happens when a teacher/trainer judges a student in terms of one, or very few, characteristics. The characteristics used to make the judgement may be entirely irrelevant to the situation – for example their gender or sexuality, disability or race. The characteristics come to determine the teacher/trainer's whole attitude to the student.

Although labelling theory originates from the study of deviancy, it has been used to examine interaction in the classroom – offering an *interactionist* approach within the sociology of education. The approach has questioned some basic issues concerning achievement in education. It is often argued that it is the students' life outside the classroom/institution that determines their success or otherwise. The interactionist approaches remind us of the dynamic nature of life *within* the learning environment and the part that practitioners and their attitudes play in determining outcomes.

References

Giddens A (1989) *Sociology* Polity Press
Giddens A (1997) *Sociology* 3rd edn Polity Press
Marsh I *et al.* (1996) *Making sense of society: an introduction to sociology* Falmer Press
McNeill P (1981) 'Language' in P McNeill & C Townley (1984) *Fundamentals of sociology* Hutchinson

6.   Access and Opportunity in PCET

Ann Lahiff

It is quite clear that not all members of our society have equal access to educational services and institutions. The readings in this section explore issues arising from this differential access in terms of class, gender, sexuality, race and ethnicity, and disability.

Social class and patterns of differentiation

> *Social strata are groupings defined in terms of their ownership of, or access to, social wealth. Social wealth refers to anything which is relatively scarce in society and which has a value, from wealth, property and income, power and influence, through health and ... education...*

> (Reid, 1996: 2)

Social class has been seen as a fundamental form of social stratification in our society, and sociologists have spent much of their time defining it. Whilst there are continued discussions surrounding the exact nature of social class, in studies of educational opportunity, access and achievement, social class is generally presented in terms of occupational groupings. The assumption underpinning this is that professional and managerial employees, for example, will have similar ownership of, or access to, social wealth (as defined by Reid, above), when contrasted with unskilled manual workers.

Although more and more people have had experience of extended education beyond 16, educational achievement continues to be systematically related to social class. Studies which compare social class origins (the class into which we are born) with destinations (the class we achieve) confirm the pivotal role that social class background plays. For example:

> *The proportion of adults who possessed a degree at the beginning of the 1990s ranged from 32% for those whose fathers were professionals, to 6% or less for men and women whose fathers were in manual or personal service work.*

> (Bilton *et al.* 1996: 343)

For many young people coming into our colleges the lack of access to adequate financial resources and to domestic surroundings conducive to learning is a considerable problem. The following account of a piece of research carried out by Inge Bates demonstrates – through a comparison of two college groups, BTEC fashion design students and YTS trainees – the crucial influence that family background and parental support have on selection of the course of study and on progress through it.

Social class and family background

The impact of gender on young people's career paths varies dramatically between social classes and, more subtly, across class fractions (see Anyon, 1983; Aggleton, 1987; Brown, 1987). The distinctive, but on the whole unrealistic, career aspirations of the fashion design students, raised the question of what sorts of social backgrounds had nurtured their aspirations. While gender operated as a general influence ... it intermingled with other social factors. First impressions of fashion design students suggested they came from rather more comfortable homes than Youth Training Scheme (YTS) trainees. However, details of parents' occupations revealed that both groups recruited largely from the working class, although the fashion design group was more socially heterogeneous, drawing students from 'upper' working-class and 'lower' middle-class backgrounds. In one student's words: 'There are no roughs and no really brainy ones. We're sort of in-between.' Or, as another explained, 'we're not loaded and we're not scrubbers'. Typical examples of fathers' occupations were fitter, plumber, clerk at the town hall and garage owner; if mothers were employed, they were mainly in secretarial work. There were occasional students from wealthy families whose fathers owned or were employed in larger companies but no students with parents who had higher education or were in professional careers. A large proportion of students' fathers were 'self-made' small businessmen, e.g. a joiner, a garage owner, an owner of a small firm selling suspended ceilings. The range of family backgrounds considered here suggests that this was a group originating in the working class but upwardly mobile over one or two generations... In all groups, but particularly the BTEC groups, there was a significant proportion of students aiming to develop their own business, suggesting the possibility that enterprise values may be distinctive to and transmitted through 'enterprising' class fractions.

The most crucial difference, however, between the YTS 'care girls' and the fashion design students was the extent to which they enjoyed particular forms of material and psychological support from their families. To risk overstating the case, in the words of one student, life at home was typically 'fairly hunky-dory'. It was this factor which enabled these students to contemplate the several years of training which it could take to become a qualified fashion designer and which also cushioned them from the need to compromise their ambitions in the face of labour market realities.

The most basic form of support was financial and it was effectively a precondition to entering the course that students' families were at least 'comfortably off'. At sixteen, few were able to claim grants and the grants which were available did not by any means cover maintenance. Consequently, families had to be willing and able to support 16-year-olds for at least two further years for them to be able to contemplate entry into a vocational course in further education, as opposed to YTS with its allowance. This clearly discriminated against families where there were financial difficulties and a need for young adult members to begin contributing to the family income. The costs of supporting students in further education did not stop with their upkeep. Costs of equipment and travel which were part of the course were estimated by these students as being in the region of £500:

Continued...

They paid for both my London trips and any other day trips we had. The initial kits at the beginning of the course came to about £100. When you add up all your books and things like that, fabric and stuff it's probably nearer £500 than £250... It is a lot.

The extent of financial support available from parents could also be a factor in work performance during the course and could influence students' attitudes to carrying on, for example, into higher education. Work performance could easily be affected by the need to take part-time jobs, as one student with three such jobs explained:

I used to start back at Baltimore at 6, then I used to get home again at 4 [a.m.] and I used to get up again and go to the Pizza Hut for 11, and I used to work at Pizza Hut from 11 to 6, come home for an hour and then go back to Baltimore and then get home at 4 [a.m.] and then get up again for college! Every evening I worked and I ended up not doing my college work ... and falling asleep at college... My tutor says to me 'you're gonna have to do something' and I said 'well I need money to do the course'.

The availability of physical space at home for college work was an additional, perhaps less obvious, condition for successfully undertaking the course. The quantity of college work meant that much had to be done at home which, for fashion design students, entailed laying out patterns and materials for making up. Some families gave up a dining room or spare bedroom especially for this purpose. It is difficult to imagine, however, how such work could be regularly undertaken within the cramped space of a council flat or small house where there might be shared bedrooms and one main living area. One student on the course described such difficulties:

I can't work at home. There's nowhere to work 'cos me bedroom's too small, it's not got a desk in it so any sewing I've got to do ... is on the dining room table and it's awkward because my brothers come in at different times so the only time you can start really sewing is after 9 o'clock at night if they've gone out.

This particular student eventually overcame this problem by working at a friend's house where there was much more space.

While material factors were important, psychological support and a stable family context were also major influences on entry into this trajectory. Comparison between background data on the fashion designers with similar data from the 'care girls' study vividly highlighted the reasons for this.

Care girls' home background example
I.B.: And your dad works shifts in the steel works?

Anne: Yes. Twelve hour nights, five nights a week... He's so tired. I don't know how he can do it... Saturday he sleeps in, he's up at four and he can't do it. He's too old now, he's 53. It's too much.

I.B.: Can he do anything about it?

Anne: Me and my mum get upset when we see him crawling in ... you know if my dad's upset, I'm upset. If my dad's poorly, I roar [cry]. I right worry about him...

Continued...

I.B.: So things aren't easy at home?

Anne: Sometimes I think, I feel like crying, I hate myself and I hate mum but then I think well I'm luckier than a lot of people, there's child abuse, there's kids getting beaten up, there's husbands battering wives... My brother, he'll say why don't you leave home? You've got all these pressures on you, just leave, just turn your back and leave, and I says to him, I says, 'I can't turn my back on my family, it's alright for you'.

I.B.: So you won't leave home very easily?

Anne: No. Turn my back on my family, no.

Fashion designers' home background example

D.H.: Have your parents supported you then while you've been at college?

Nancy: Well, they've always been there if I've needed to talk, if I've had any problems and they've helped me a lot with money, you know ... they paid for my first college trip to London... They've just always been around to help me... And they've took me to places to do questionnaires and surveys and things [for BTEC projects].

D.H.: They've helped you practically?

Nancy: My mum's helped me out with me work, you know she's done a bit of hand-sewing for me or whatever and cut out me fabric for me when I've been really pushed. Everybody's helped in fact. You know ... even little Dale's stapled things together for me ... we have a really good time.

D.H.: Where do you do your work at home?

Nancy: Everyone just helps out and I've had me fabric laid all over the floor ... it's been good. They've always been quiet when I've been working or just helped me out... They've moved all the furniture, took everything up and just let me have all the space. They've been great.

The two young women were in quite opposite family situations. Anne was burdened by problems linked with her father's need to carry on with shift-working to avoid redundancy, his ill-health and associated family tensions. The problems were such that she also felt trapped, needed by the family and unable to 'turn her back' on them. Her accounts were typical of those given by the 'care girls', which were frequently laden with descriptions of unemployment difficulties, ill-health and conflict, leading the girls to a position of feeling desperate to leave home or alternatively bound to stay. In Nancy's family, dependency relations were completely reversed. Nancy felt that her parents and family assisted her both psychologically and practically in her training and her career. Whereas Nancy's success in going to college floated on a supportive sub-structure of family life, Anne suffered the worry that her family would 'sink' without her.

While Nancy was perhaps a little exceptional in the degree of support she drew from her family, the majority of students on this course indicated that their parents were on the whole encouraging and helpful and took a definite interest in their college training and their careers:

And so I had a talk with my mum and dad, they said, look it's up to you, we want what's best for you, we don't mind if you're not going to get a grant at college you know, we'll support you in whatever you do...

Continued...

80

Well I come from a family where me mum and dad are bothered about what I do, they don't just say 'oh go away and do whatever you want'. That's why they wanted me to do A levels 'cos they knew it would stand me in good stead.

But they're like behind me all the way. You know like they know it's what I want to do and I want two years experience and saying that, 'you've just got to go wherever education is'.

I think mum and dad are happy about it really 'cos like everybody else they just went into a job, you know, and me dad always said, 'get as much qualifications as you can 'cos there's better jobs and things'.

What their parents appeared to offer was generalized, unconditional support for further education and training. They wanted their youngsters to get 'as much qualifications as you can' but were undiscriminating about the related career prospects. Further questioning of the students suggested that their parents had little knowledge of career opportunities in fashion design and could not assess the realism of their children's goals.

These perspectives also had a class-gendered dimension. There was some evidence that in these families realistic career prospects were considered a less significant issue for girls than for boys:

My brother's doing computing... I don't know what they would have said if he'd wanted to go in for fashion design ... but he wouldn't have wanted to.

My dad thinks I'd have been better off doing a secretarial type course, but he thinks I'll get married anyway.

On the whole, intrinsic satisfaction figured more prominently than extrinsic rewards in parents' assumptions about what was most likely to prove important in girls' careers. In summary, social class and family background influenced entry into fashion design training both through the transmission of enterprise values and through their capacity to raise what would otherwise have been financial, spatial and psychological barriers to extended vocational training in this field. The particular quality of family supportiveness which the students tended to enjoy was, however, a mixed blessing, particularly in the context of the gendered 'career myopia' mentioned above. While these students' parents were keen to encourage their youngsters to continue their education and struggled in various ways to support them, they were culturally naive and not overly concerned about the value and status of different types of qualifications and different forms of education and training. Partly as a consequence of this, their daughters' ambitions developed in a 'greenhouse' environment, which fostered career dreams far removed from labour market realities.

References

Aggleton P (1987) *Rebels without a cause* Falmer Press

Anyon J (1993) 'Intersections of class and gender' in S Walker & L Barton (eds) *Gender, class and education* Falmer Press

Brown P (1987) *Schooling ordinary kids* Tavistock

(Bates, 1993: 72–77)

Some writers have linked social class to what they describe as *cultural deprivation*. In the next reading Tony Bilton explores this issue.

Cultural deprivation

Theories of cultural deprivation focus not upon the innate qualities of particular social groups, but upon their *cultural inheritance*. Children who are 'culturally deprived' may be bright enough, but held back by values and attitudes that are not conducive to educational success.

In the early post-war period, theories of cultural deprivation were often used in connection with social class. Bernstein (1971) argued that the reliance by many working-class families on a 'restricted code' of speech made it more difficult for working-class children to undertake abstract analytical work. Other theorists targeted other aspects of working-class culture, among them an inability to defer gratification, lack of parental interest in children's education, and a lack of ambition.

Since the 1970s, it is black and Asian pupils who are more often said to be culturally deprived. Theorists have proposed a range of cultural obstacles to educational success, from the prevalence of 'mother-centred' families to lack of parental interest, from low self-esteem to the tensions of culture clash. Many of these suggestions have been effectively discounted; for example, Brah & Minhas (1988) refute the widespread notion that the education of Asian girls suffers from the tensions of mediating two contradictory cultures, the 'liberal' culture of the school and the 'repressive' culture of home. There is no evidence, they point out, of greater intergenerational conflict in Asian families than there is within other communities; the culture clash argument is based on misleading and ethnocentric comparisons... But as a type of explanation, theories of cultural deprivation continue to flourish...

Deprivation in culture, society and education

[We would argue] against those theories that seem to reduce culture to a lifestyle choice, and then to 'blame' under-achieving groups for making the 'wrong' decision. A more sophisticated view recognises that values that affect educational decisions – commitment to education as a strategy for advancement, willingness to play the game – are not attitudes which can simply be dropped or acquired, but are rooted instead in the shared experiences of working and community life and, indeed, in the experiences of schooling itself.

There is not room here to consider the socio-linguistic theories of Basil Bernstein in detail, but his work on the acquisition of skills and competencies, on experience and modes of control, attempts to examine how the realities of working-class and middle-class life encourage different sorts of skills and interests. He and his colleagues find, for example, that, while many working-class mothers regard play and learning as separate activities (a view that reflects the nature of manual occupations), middle-class mothers tend to view toys and play as opportunities for enquiry; it is possible that middle-class mothers enable their children to take explicit educational advantage from play. Middle-class children, then, may arrive at school with advantages in two respects: they may indeed have learned more as a result of their socialisation, and their expectations may be more in line with those of the school. It

Continued...

---

is useful to conceive of the competencies and experiences that may be more prevalent in middle-class households as resources, resources that are differentially distributed throughout the class structure, and that may be of concrete advantage to children who receive them. Inheritance, it has been said, can be 'cultural' as well as financial.

However, a problem with this type of formulation – as with cultural deprivation theory – is that it tends to take for granted a single model of the educable child – primarily white and middle class. The educational failure of certain groups is then 'explained' by the degree to which they deviate from this model. But instead of asserting that children who do not conform to the model are less well prepared for school, we could as easily argue that the school is less well prepared for them – that the education system is insufficiently responsive to their gifts and their needs.

References

Bernstein B (1971) 'A critique of the concept of compensatory education' in *Class, codes and conduct, vol 1* Routledge & Kegan Paul

Brah A & Minhas R (1988) 'Structural racism or cultural difference: schooling for Asian girls' in M Woodhead & A McGrath (eds) *Family, school and society* Hodder & Stoughton

(Bilton, 1996: 352; 356)

The way in which one group of schoolboys engaged with the culture of their school – or rather clashed with it – is described in the field-study outlined in the next extract from Giddens.

Education and cultural reproduction

Cultural reproduction refers to the ways in which schools, in conjunction with other social institutions, help perpetuate social and economic inequalities across the generations. The concept directs our attention to the means whereby, via the hidden curriculum, schools influence the learning of values, attitudes and habits. Schools reinforce variations in cultural values and outlooks picked up early in life; when children leave school, these have the effect of limiting the opportunities of some, while facilitating those of others.

The modes of language-use identified by Bernstein no doubt connect to such broad cultural differences, which underlie variations in interests and tastes. Children from lower-class backgrounds, particularly those from minority groups, develop ways of talking and acting which clash with those dominant in the school. As Bowles & Gintis emphasize, schools impose rules of discipline upon pupils, the authority of teachers being oriented towards academic learning. Working-class children experience a much greater cultural clash when they enter school than those from more privileged homes. The former find themselves in effect in a foreign cultural environment. Not only are they less likely to be motivated towards high academic performance; their habitual modes of speech and action, as Bernstein holds, do not mesh with those of the teachers, even if each is trying their best to communicate.

Continued...

Children spend long hours in school. As Illich stresses, they learn much more there than is contained in the lessons they are actually taught. Children get an early taste of what the world of work will be like, learning that they are expected to be punctual and apply themselves diligently to the tasks which those in authority set for them (Webb & Westergaard, 1991).

Willis: an analysis of cultural reproduction

A celebrated discussion of cultural reproduction is provided in the report of a field-work study carried out by Paul Willis in a school in Birmingham (Willis, 1977). The question he set out to investigate was how cultural reproduction occurs – or, as he puts it, 'how working-class kids get working-class jobs'. It is often thought that, during the process of schooling, children from lower-class or minority backgrounds simply come to see that they 'are not clever enough' to expect to get highly paid or high-status jobs in their future work lives. In other words, the experience of academic failure teaches them to recognize their intellectual limitations; having accepted their 'inferiority', they move into occupations with limited career prospects.

As Willis points out, this interpretation does not conform at all to the reality of people's lives and experiences. The 'street wisdom' of those from poor neighbourhoods may be of little or no relevance to academic success, but involves as subtle, skilful and complex a set of abilities as any of the intellectual skills taught in school. Few if any children leave school thinking 'I'm so stupid that it's fair and proper for me to be stacking boxes in a factory all day'. If children from less privileged backgrounds accept menial jobs, without feeling themselves throughout life to be failures, there must be other factors involved.

Willis concentrated on a particular boys' group in the school, spending a lot of time with them. The members of the gang, who called themselves 'the lads', were white; the school also contained many children from West Indian and Asian backgrounds. Willis found that the lads had an acute and perceptive understanding of the school's authority system – but used this to fight that system rather than working with it. They saw the school as an alien environment, but one which they could manipulate to their own ends. They derived positive pleasure from the constant conflict – which they kept mostly to minor skirmishes – they carried on with teachers. They were adept at seeing the weak points of the teachers' claims to authority, as well as where they were vulnerable as individuals.

In class, for instance, the children were expected to sit still, be quiet and get on with their work. But the lads were all movement, save when the teacher's stare might freeze one of them momentarily; they would gossip surreptitiously, or pass open remarks that were on the verge of direct subordination but could be explained away if challenged. Willis describes all this beautifully:

'The lads' specialise in a caged resentment which always stops just short of outright confrontation. Settled in class, as near a group as they can manage, there is a continuous scraping of chairs, a bad-tempered 'tut-tutting' at the simplest request, and a continuous fidgeting about which explores every permutation of sitting or lying on a chair. During private study, some openly show disdain by

Continued...

84

apparently trying to go to sleep with their heads sideways down on the desk, some have their backs to the desk gazing out of the window, or even vacantly at the wall... A continuous hum of talk flows around injunctions not to, like the inevitable tide over barely dried sand, and everywhere there are rolled-back eyeballs and exaggerated mutterings of conspiratorial secrets... In the corridors there is a foot-dragging walk, an over-friendly 'hello' or sudden silence as the deputy [senior teacher] passes. Derisive or insane laughter erupts which might or might not be about someone who has just passed. It is as demeaning to stop as it is to carry on... Opposition to the school is principally manifested in the struggle to win symbolic and physical space from the institution and its rules and to defeat its main perceived purpose: to make you 'work'.

(Willis, 1977: 12–13; 26)

The lads referred to conformist children – those who accepted the authority of the teachers, and concerned themselves with academic values – as 'the ear-'oles'. The ear-'oles actually *listened* to the teachers, and did as they were told. The ear-'oles would go on to be far more 'successful', in terms of getting well-paid, comfortable jobs on leaving school, than the lads. Yet their awareness of the complexities of the school environment, according to Willis, was in many respects less profound than that of the lads. They accepted them in an unquestioning way.

Most pupils were somewhere between the lads on the one side and the ear-'oles on the other – less openly confrontational than the first group, and less consistently conformist than the second. Styles and modes of opposition, however, were also strongly influenced by ethnic divisions. The teachers were mostly white, and in spite of their distaste for the school, the lads had more in common with them than black children did. Some groups of children from West Indian families were much more openly, and violently, hostile to the school than the lads. The lads themselves were openly racist, and distinguished themselves sharply from the black gangs.

The lads recognized that work would be much like school, but they actively looked forward to it. They expected to gain no direct satisfaction from the work environment, but were impatient for wages. Far from taking the jobs they did – in tyre-fitting, carpet-laying, plumbing, painting and decorating – from feelings of inferiority, they held an attitude of dismissive superiority towards work, as they had towards school. They enjoyed the adult status which came from working, but were uninterested in 'making a career' for themselves.

As Willis points out, work in blue-collar settings often involves quite similar cultural features to those the lads created in their counter-school culture – banter, quick wit, and the skill to subvert the demands of authority figures where necessary. Only later in their lives might they come to see themselves as trapped in arduous, unrewarding labour. When they have families, they might perhaps look back on education retrospectively – and hopelessly – as the only escape. Yet if they try to pass this view on to their own children, they are likely to have no more success than their own parents did.

Continued...

References

Webb R & Westergaard H (1991) 'Social stratification: culture and education'
Sociology Review 1

Willis P (1977) *Learning to labour: how working class kids get working class jobs*
Saxon House

(Giddens, 1997: 417–419)

Gender and patterns of differentiation

There is much evidence now that girls are overtaking boys in educational achievement. The next extract, from Pamela Abbott & Claire Wallace, identifies where differentiation still occurs and offers accounts which may explain this.

Girls' educational achievements

Girls now generally do better than boys in school, as measured by passes in school examinations – GCSE and GCE A levels; as girls and women have been granted more equal access to education so they have caught up with boys and men at each level, and at some levels they are now overtaking them. Young women obtain better results in 16+ examinations than boys, and they are overtaking them at A level GCE as well. In 1991/2 31.4 per cent of females obtained one or more A levels as against 27.8 per cent of males...

Female enrolments are fast catching up with male enrolments in higher education too. Although the numbers in higher education in general have grown during the 1980s and 1990s, the biggest growth has been amongst women; there are now two-and-a-half times more women in the system than in 1970/1. Indeed, in terms of applications to university in 1994/5, there were more female applicants than male ones...

Even in post-graduate education, numbers of women going on to further degrees have increased dramatically since 1980. In 1970/1 there were twice as many male post-graduate students as female, but by 1992/3 there were only 11 per cent more (CSO, 1995). Department for Education estimates for 1994/5 (May 1995) indicate that for the first time there are more full-time female students actually on first degrees than male ones – 324.1 thousands compared with 320.6 thousands. (Men still outnumber women as full-time post-graduate students – 43.1 thousands compared to 35.8 thousands – and on non-degree full-time programmes – 58.6 thousands compared with 56.3 thousands.)

More girls stay in full-time education after the age of 16 than boys, although boys are more likely to have day release from an employer – reflecting the small number of girls who are taken on as apprentices. Women are more likely than men to take evening classes. Why do women do so well within the education system?

One answer is that achievement and conformity at school contradict certain codes of masculinity, especially working-class masculinity (Willis, 1977). Additionally, the

Continued...

greater surveillance of girls and young women by parents also pushes them into doing homework. Girls are denied the freedom to 'go out' in the evenings that is extended to their brothers, and they tend to spend at least some of the time doing their homework. This differential policing of boys and girls and the ways in which it encourages girls to do homework is particularly evident in the fact that girls meet the deadlines for GCSE coursework which boys often miss (Gwen Wallace, 1996)... Some research has suggested that Asian girls may be particularly disadvantaged by the amount of domestic labour they are required to perform (Wallace, 1996), and other research (Bates, 1993) has indicated that girls may be expected to take time off school for housework and child care.

Women tend to become qualified in different subjects from men. For example, women outnumber men at A level in domestic subjects, languages, English, art/craft/design and history. Men outnumber women in technical drawing, natural sciences, computer studies, geography and maths. This same pattern emerges in higher education... There are twice as many women as men in the arts and twice as many men as women in the sciences. In social sciences the numbers are evenly spread, but this again changes when we look more precisely at which subjects are being pursued – men are strongly represented in law and economics, women in sociology and psychology...

A study by Kim Thomas (1990) looked at how different subjects in higher education are gendered. She compared undergraduates in physics and English/communications studies and looked at the different experiences of men and women in each subject area. She found that sciences were seen as embodying hard, incontrovertible and necessary knowledge leading to more serious, well-rewarded and prestigious careers. Scientists saw themselves in a 'subject hierarchy' above 'vague and wishy-washy' subjects such as humanities. The minority of women who studied such 'hard' sciences were very determined to succeed but nevertheless felt marginalised in the male-dominated and competitive world of sciences. They were likely to see their career goals as conflicting with family goals if they were to marry. They were never seen as totally successful within physics and were often nonconformist in their behaviour within the science establishment. By comparison, only a small number of students of English were men but although this was seen as a more vague, indeterminate and 'feminine' subject in the hierarchy of university values, men who behaved in an assertive, individualistic way with strong opinions were able to do very well. Here it was the men who tended to be more nonconformist. Thomas concludes that subjects were gendered in very particular ways and that masculinity and femininity took different forms within them.

It is interesting to note that women graduates are more likely to be in paid employment than women who completed only compulsory education – and this is true across the European Union. In Britain in 1991, for example, 90 per cent of women aged 20–39 without children younger than 18 were in paid employment, but 94 per cent of those with degrees. The difference for those with children is more startling – 56 per cent compared with 74 per cent. Graduate mothers are also more likely to be employed full time than non-graduate mothers (CEC, 1993).

Continued...

It is also necessary to look at what happens to non-academic girls. Here it is evident that their main education is preparation for 'women's jobs'. Their aspirations are 'cooled out' not just by educational failure but also by the expectations of their future roles in the family. Many parents, teachers and employers ask: 'What is the point of girls striving for success at school when they will only get married and become dependants of men?' as do some girls themselves (Lees, 1993). Such expectations filter through to the girls, and domestic roles are seen as the alternative to academic success for them. In reality they are likely to spend much of their lives in paid work, so this experience in the education system leaves them ready to accept lower-paid, lower-status jobs without promotion prospects. However, there has been something of a shift in attitudes. Research by Sue Sharpe (1995) suggests that while in the past young women saw marriage and motherhood as an inevitability and the latter as necessitating a break in their working life, they now expect to have jobs, babies *and* husband. Rather than marriage and motherhood being seen as an alternative career, it is seen as a parallel career. However, Sue Lees (1993) argues that while academic girls expect careers, non-academic girls anticipate part-time employment taken to 'fit in' with child care and domestic responsibilities. Mirza (1992) found that the Black girls she interviewed anticipated a career, but this was in marked contrast to the Irish girls in the study, who saw their futures as home-makers, child-carers and part-time workers. For these girls domestic fulfilment and commitment to the full-time labour market were seen to be incompatible.

In order to understand women's situation in the education system it is necessary to understand how gender interacts with ethnicity. What is evident is that Asian and West Indian women tend to have fewer academic qualifications than white women. However, West Indian women are more likely than West Indian men to have obtained GCSE grades A–C, to have vocational qualifications (a large percentage in nursing) (Mirza, 1992), and their performance is improving relative to their white peers. Furthermore, Afro-American women are also likely to be the higher achievers in continuing education in the USA (Mickelson, 1992). But in Britain, Asian women in the 16–24 age-group are much more likely than Asian men to have no academic qualifications (Brown, 1985). Therefore the way in which women perform relative to men in the educational system varies according to ethnicity (as does the value of having or not having educational qualifications)...

Explaining girls' continued disadvantage

Christine Skelton (1993) has pointed out that girls' educational experience is different from and unequal to that of boys:

> *Whether the focus of research has been on female pupils, teachers/lecturers or students in further and higher education, the findings have all illustrated how females receive and perceive different messages about their aptitudes and abilities from those of males, which has implications for their place in the family and the labour market.*

> (Skelton, 1993: 324)

Sandra Acker (1994) has indicated that feminists are not solely or mainly concerned with issues of achievement. She suggests that it is now indisputable that girls

Continued...

perform as well as, if not better than, boys in formal schooling. The debate is more complex however, it is about differential curricula: the avoidance by girls of science and technology; sexual harassment; the career prospects of women teachers and lecturers; the unequal treatment by teachers of boys and girls; and the weaving of gender differentials into the very fabric of school life (Acker, 1994). She suggests that there is a 'hidden curriculum' of gender differentiation that continues to operate and influence school processes despite the apparent gender neutrality of the official curriculum.

First, the academic hierarchy remains very firmly masculine. The higher up the academic ladder we go, the more dominated it becomes by men. Primary and infant schools are more likely to have women teachers and women heads. At the other end of the spectrum, there are far fewer women professors than male ones and hardly any female vice-chancellors or college principals. Women are concentrated at the bottom rungs of the professional ladder within colleges, and this applies equally to any level of the educational system at which we choose to look... Female teachers are ... concentrated in posts as classroom teachers and less frequently found in promoted posts. Teaching provides a job for female teachers but the potential of a career for men. The situation is even more stark in higher education, where during 1991–2 women comprised roughly one fifth of full-time academic staff but only about 5 per cent of professors (Acker, 1994). This means that the role models which boys and girls have available are ones suggesting that positions of high prestige are taken by men, reinforcing roles elsewhere in society...

Second, feminists have demonstrated that teachers have stereotyped attitudes to boys and girls and that the school reinforces rather than challenges gender divisions in the wider world. Ann-Marie Wolpe (1977) has argued that girls are encouraged to behave in a feminine way, and teachers see it as part of their duty to inculcate properly feminine standards of behaviour; more recently (1989) she has argued that in order to bring about change in girls' education it will be necessary to review and restructure the whole educational system systematically. Michelle Stanworth (1983) found, in her study of a humanities department in a further education college, that in an A level class there was a tendency for both boys and girls to underestimate girls' academic performance and to regard the boys as more capable and more intelligent. Male teachers, when asked what they thought their pupils would be doing in future, tended to see even the most able female pupils' futures in terms of marriage, children and domesticity. When careers for girls were mentioned they tended to be sex-stereotypical personal assistants and secretaries – even when these were not what the girls themselves wanted. However, the male pupils were seen as having careers ahead of them, with marriage hardly mentioned. This expectation of the teachers was in turn reflected in the expectations of pupils. Stanworth found that teachers seemed to be heavily influenced by the verbal contributions that pupils made in the class when making judgements about their academic ability, as were the pupils when making judgements about each other. The teachers agreed with the opinion of boys that they were more able than the girls and based this judgement on verbal contributions in the class, as the boys rarely had access to the girls' marks. This was despite the fact that some of the girls consistently got better marks for the written work than did the boys...

Continued...

Third, textbooks embody various assumptions about gender identities... School textbooks and history curricula, with their emphasis on factual knowledge of key people and political development in Britain, perpetuate bias and influence students' interpretation of and attitude towards women in general by marginalising and ignoring their role...

Fourth, although most schools are now co-educational, gender differentiation is nevertheless reflected in the organisation of the school – gender differentiation is a fact of life in schools. The outcome of gender differentiation is that while girls, especially in primary schools, are the 'model' pupils, both they and boys come to see boys as more important and to accept that it is boys/men who must be prioritised and who ultimately have authority...

Research in secondary schools has also demonstrated boys' domination of the classroom and teacher time (Lees, 1993). At secondary school it is also argued that girls and boys develop subject preferences that prepare them for their future roles. Until the introduction of the National Curriculum the choices that girls made in the secondary school, as well as parental and teacher expectations (Kelly, 1982) and the ways in which the timetable and subject choices were organised (Pratt, 1984), prepared girls for 'female' jobs and domesticity. Traditional careers advice and teachers' attitudes tended to mean that girls did not choose science subjects; it is often suggested that girls are uneasy in handling science equipment and that they lack the familiarity with it that boys often have... The statistical evidence on girls taking science subjects at school and in higher education indicates that, despite a number of initiatives designed to encourage girls into science and engineering, there was little change between the early 1980s and the 1990s. While the proportion of girls taking chemistry and physics A levels increased marginally, it actually declined in biology – the only science A level taken by more girls than boys (Shelley & Whaley, 1994). In higher education in 1993 young men outnumbered young women by 6 to 1 in engineering and technology, 3 to 1 in mathematical sciences, architecture and related skills and 2 to 1 in the physical sciences (Acker, 1994).

Judy Wajcman (1994) has indicated that the proportion of women taking computer courses in higher education has declined in the last twenty years, while at the same time information technology has become widely used in schools. She argues that access to computing at home and in schools is dominated by boys, that computing has become sex-stereotyped. She concludes that 'the absence of technical confidence or competence does indeed become part of the female gender identity as well as being a sexual stereotype'...

Other researchers have suggested that science and technology teachers see girls as deficient, as lacking the necessary aptitude to do science and technology (Versey, 1990). However, the accumulating evidence is that the 'ability' to do science and technology has more to do with the differential opportunities that girls and boys have to tinker and play with construction toys and the gender stereotyping of subjects as 'boys' and 'girls' areas (Harte, 1992). Volman & Van Ecke (1995) suggest that the problem needs to be reconceptualised – away from seeing girls as the problem and towards seeing science and technology as the problem. The attitudes of girls to

Continued...

science and technology do not reflect misunderstanding or prejudice, but social realities...

Fifth, there are different kinds of classroom interaction associated with the different genders. Detailed analysis of the moment-to-moment interaction in the classroom indicates that boys talk more and are allowed to dominate the classroom interaction, and this continues even when teachers are consciously trying to overcome it (Spender, 1982). Skelton (1989) has suggested that teachers typically work to interest boys for the sake of maintaining order. Goddard-Spear (1990) argues that boys are perceived as more active learners than girls, dominate teachers' time and are regarded more highly by teachers. Feminist researchers have pointed to the importance of language in the classroom. They have drawn attention to the tendency of girls to take a back seat in the classroom and to be more hesitant in making contributions than boys. Girls are often reluctant to speak in class, and diminished in the discussion which takes place. The classroom becomes seen as a man's world and girls are marginalised...

Taken together, these indirect forms of socialisation are sometimes called 'the hidden curriculum'. While the overt message may be that the expectation of girls and boys is the same, this is subverted by a different message underlying the curriculum.

References

Acker S (1994) *Gendered education* Open University Press

Bates I (1993) 'A job which is "right for me"?' in I Bates & G Riseborough (eds) *Youth and inequality* Open University Press

Brown C (1985) *Black and white Britain* Gower

CEC (1993) *Employment in Britain* Commission of the European Community

CSO (Central Statistical Office) (1995) *Social trends 25* HMSO

Goddard-Spear M (1990) 'Differences between the written work of boys and girls' *British Educational Research Journal* 15, pp271–277

Kelly A (1982) 'Gender roles at home and school' *British Journal of Sociology of Education* 3, pp281–296

Lees S (1993) *Sugar and spice: sexuality and adolescent girls* Penguin

Mickelson RA (1992) 'Why does Jane read and write so well? The anomaly of women's achievement' in J Wrigley (ed) *Education and gender inequality* Falmer

Mirza H (1992) *Young, female and black* Routledge

Pratt J (1984) *Option choice: a question of equal opportunity* NFER/Nelson

Sharpe S (1995) *Just like a girl* 2nd edn Penguin

Shelley V & Whaley P (1994) 'Women in science: access, experience and progression' in BR Singh (ed) *Improving gender and ethnic relations* Cassell

Skelton C (ed) (1989) *Whatever happens to little women?* Open University Press

Skelton C (1993) 'Women and education' in D Richardson & V Robinson (eds) *Introducing women's studies: feminist theory and practice* Macmillan

Spender D (1982) *Invisible women: the schooling scandal* Writers' and Readers' Publishing Cooperative

Stanworth M (1983) *Gender and schooling: a case study of sexual division in the classroom* Hutchinson

Continued...

Thomas K (1990) *Gender and subject in HE* Open University Press

Versey J (1990) 'Taking action on gender issues in science education' *School Science Review* 71, p256

Volman M & Van Ecke E (1995) 'Girls in science and technology: the development of a discourse' *Gender and Education* 7, pp283–292

Wajcman J (1994) 'Technology as a masculine culture' in *The Polity reader in gender studies* Polity

Wallace G (1996) Personal communication, based on 'Making your way through secondary school' research project

Willis P (1977) *Learning to labour: how working class kids get working class jobs* Saxon House

Wolpe A-M (1977) *Some processes in education: explorations in feminism* Women's Research & Resource Centre

Wolpe A-M (1989) *Within school walls: the role of discipline, sexuality and the curriculum* Routledge & Kegan Paul

(Abbott & Wallace, 1997: 85–90; 93–101)

From the discussions presented in the extracts from Abbott & Wallace, it is clear that common assumptions about 'what it means to be a woman' (the concept of femininity) and 'what it means to be a man' (the concept of masculinity), impact upon the choices young people make both on entering post-16 education and training and in their aspirations for employment. However, to appreciate fully the ways in which gender impacts on the learning experience, we need to acknowledge the extent to which the definitions of masculinity and femininity in our society are implicitly *heterosexual*. A consideration of the impact of sexuality on learning now follows.

Sexuality and the learning experience

The sexualities of students and teachers/trainers have an impact on the nature of the learning experience in PCET. In much the same way that gender can determine both learner expectations and tutor-student interaction, so can sexuality. As has been seen above, understandings of the key concepts of masculinity and femininity play a great part in forming both teachers' expectations of learners and learners' expectations of themselves and their peers. But it is important to recognise how these key concepts are built around assumptions of heterosexual behaviour.

To consider the assumptions, consider the following brief quote from Jones & Mahony (1989):

A parent at a parents' meeting expressed the fear that the school's policy of widening employment opportunities for both sexes would 'turn kids queer'.

While applauding the school's attempts to encourage girls into science and technology, we have to be careful not to give the impression that we're wanting to turn out a lot of butch engineers. (School Governor at a Governors' meeting)

I really wanted to retrain to teach Home Economics, but I got so much hassle, I dropped it. Everyone thought I'd gone gay. (Male teacher)

Jones & Mahony go on to make explicit the links between employment opportunities and sexuality:

> *Just from these three quotes alone, the connections between equal work opportunities and sexuality are obvious. Embedded in attitudes to what constitutes proper work for women and men are notions about what counts as being a proper man or woman, and fundamental to those concepts are questions which are ultimately about sexuality.*

Two concepts are important here – heterosexism and homophobia:

1. *Heterosexism*: A set of beliefs, attitudes and practices which presents and promotes heterosexual relationships and lifestyles as the norm. It therefore sees such relationships as superior and in many cases considers alternatives as unacceptable and unnatural.

2. *Homophobia*: Fear and/or hatred of homosexuality, which may or may not be manifested overtly.

The set of beliefs, attitudes and practices upon which heterosexism and homophobia are based, serve to regulate and control behaviour. Difference is spurned and ridiculed rather than celebrated. Most homophobic abuse or remarks are directed not (just) at lesbians and gay men, but at any young woman or man, girl or boy, who does not conform to the behavioural stereotypes which are deemed appropriate to their gender in the dominant culture.

The *general* effect of heterosexism and homophobia, like sexism, racism and other forms of oppression, is one of limiting possibilities for everyone. The *particular* effect on individuals in the learning environment is more extreme. The next short reading by Liz Kelly gives an indication of the damaging effect of heterosexism and homophobia on learners' educational experiences.

Lesbian and gay experience at school

We currently know very little about the experiences of young lesbians and gays in school except through exploratory studies like those of London Gay Teenage Group, and anecdotal evidence from teachers. Lorraine Trenchard and Hugh Warren (1987) surveyed 416 young people (two thirds male, predominantly white and almost half working class), all whom had faced hostility and abuse because of their sexuality. Sixty percent said that homosexuality or lesbianism was never mentioned by any of their teachers, the vast majority of cases where it had been mentioned was in a negative or unhelpful way. Only one in forty recalled it being mentioned in sex education lessons – a very different picture than that suggested by recent right-wing propaganda. Moreover, this failure to address the needs and experiences of lesbian and gay pupils had serious consequences: a strong sense of isolation; verbal abuse and teasing; for some being beaten up in school. One in five of these young people had attempted suicide.

Continued...

> *Young people were constantly exposed to uninformed and derogatory images of homosexuality and lesbianism through the media, playground talk and anti-homosexual/anti-lesbian jokes.*
>
> (Trenchard & Warren, 1987: 226)

It is this reality of having to hide, pretend, be dishonest or face taunts, hostility and worse that is never addressed by right-wing lobbyists – their remarks are couched in terms of concern for children and young people, yet they display remarkably little when those young people are lesbian or gay.

Canadian research cited by Lenskyji (1990) reported that: over a third of young lesbian and gay students had gone on heterosexual dates in an attempt to conceal their sexual identity; these young people knew more about heterosexual sex than lesbian and gay sexuality; and that the only images available to them were of 'effeminate' gay men and 'macho' lesbians. Such evidence from Britain and Canada shows that the resulting confusion, anxiety and alienation affected these young people's academic performance.

The depth of homophobia amongst some young people, particularly young men, was brought home to us in our current study through volunteered responses to a question about sexual identity. The hostility and violence in some of the young men's responses was matched only by their responses to a question about policy in relation to child abusers. Some of the spontaneous comments about lesbians and gays we recorded included: 'shoot them all'; 'put them in the gas ovens'; 'makes me sick to even think about it!'

So long as sexuality is not regarded as a basic equal opportunities issue, the only or dominant form of sexuality which is affirmed in schools is a macho male heterosexuality. The majority of students are not only excluded in the process, but are potential targets for abuse from those boys, young and adult men who choose to use this potential source of power over others.

References

Lenskyji R (1990) 'Beyond plumbing and prevention: feminist approaches to sex education' *Gender and Education* 2, pp217–230

Trenchard L & Warren H (1987) *Something to tell you* Gay Teenage Group

(Kelly, 1992: 31–32)

Gay men and lesbians are not in any sense an homogenous group. There are lesbians and gay men in every social class and ethnic group, and there are enormous variations in politics and lifestyles. There are also many lesbians and gay men with disabilities, whose existence and needs are all too often overlooked. Being prepared to recognise that not everyone you meet is heterosexual, is a small but significant starting point in your interaction with learners and colleagues in PCET. Examining your own attitudes for prejudice towards students and staff whose sexual orientation may be different from your own is a pre-requisite for developing a positive, non-threatening learning environment.

Race, ethnicity and patterns of differentiation

The literature concerning the impact of race and ethnicity on learning has largely focused on differential levels of achievement between groups. There are parallels here with the attempts to explain differential achievement of young people from different social class backgrounds. Indeed, it could be argued that while social class concerned educationalists of the 1970s, educationalists of the 1980s and 1990s have tended to focus on race and ethnicity.

Race and ethnicity are, however, confusing and much debated concepts and much of the literature takes for granted a shared understanding of the concepts. Bilton *et al.* (1996) refer to this as the 'problems of terminology' and illustrate in the following way:

> *Everyday and academic 'racial' classifications are full of ambiguities: at times groups are defined by skin colour, country of origin, descent or even by religious affiliation. Labels can appear contradictory so that, for example, the majority of 'West Indians' in Britain were actually British born. Another complication is that racial terms and classifications alter over time and are the subject of controversy and struggle. An example of this is the term 'black'. Previously seen as pejorative, it was claimed as a source of pride by African American radicals in the 1960s who rejected the classification 'coloured' then in common usage. Recently in Britain, 'black' is again the centre of dispute as Asian academics and political activists have argued over its validity as a blanket term for all non-white groups*

> (Modood, cited in Bilton *et al.* 1996: 238)

> *Disputes about the meaning and usage of words can be off-putting. It is important to ask, however, why they occur so frequently in discussions of race. That the language is uncertain, changing and, above all, political, shows that far from being natural and fixed, as they are often presented, racial and ethnic divisions are socially constructed.*

> (Bilton *et al.* 1996: 239)

Bearing Bilton's advice in mind, it is important in any analysis to have working definitions as a starting point. This should facilitate clear thinking and assist in an examination of the impact of race and ethnicity on educational experiences in PCET.

The concept of race is explored in this short extract from Giddens (1997).

Race and biology

Many people today believe – mistakenly – that humans can be readily separated into biologically different races. This is not surprising considering the numerous attempts by scholars to establish racial categorization of the peoples of the world. Some authors have distinguished four or five major races, while others have recognized as many as three dozen. But too many exceptions have been found to these classifications to make any of them workable.

Continued...

> A commonly used type, for example, Negroid, is supposed to involve dark skin, tightly curled black hair and certain other physical characteristics. Yet the original inhabitants of Australia, the Aborigines, possess dark skin but wavy, and sometimes blond, hair. A host of other examples can be found that defy any simple classifications. There are no clear-cut 'races', only a range of physical variations in human beings. Differences in physical type between groups of human beings arise from population inbreeding, which varies according to the degree of contact between different social or cultural groups. Human population groups are a continuum. The genetic diversity *within* populations that share certain visible physical traits is as great as those between them. In virtue of these facts many biologists, anthropologists and sociologists believe that the concept of race should be dropped altogether.
>
> There are clear physical differences between human beings and some of these differences are inherited. But the question of why some differences, and not others, become matters for social discrimination and prejudice has nothing to do with biology. Racial differences, therefore, should be understood as *physical variations singled out by the members of a community or society as socially significant*. Differences in skin colour, for example, are often treated as significant in this way, whereas differences in colour of hair are not. Racism is prejudice based on socially significant physical distinctions. A *racist* is someone who believes that some individuals are superior or inferior to others as a result of these racial differences.
>
> (Giddens, 1997: 212)

Advances in genetics, in particular, have confirmed that as a method of classifying people, race is based on a 'delusion'. The classifications lack scientific validity – variations within groups being as significant as those between them. Given this evidence with respect to the biology and identity, should the concept of race be used at all? Again, this is much disputed terrain but there are resolutions. Some would argue (Richardson & Lambert, 1986) that simply because the concept has little biological validity, it doesn't lose its significance. Race is thus viewed as a *'social construction'*.

> *Once people choose to attribute variable social meanings to physical differences and behave **as if** biology did fix attributes and abilities, then that becomes part of social reality. What people make of physical differences, the everyday or commonsense notions which influence them, constitutes the **social meaning of race.***
>
> (Richardson & Lambert, 1986: 14 [emphasis added])

This resolution to the question leads some sociologists and educationalists to continue to use the concept of race. This also reflects the realities of those who are subject to racism in society. Being Black or White in a racist society is the determining factor and has led many to use 'Black' and 'White' as categories of difference – irrespective of differences within Black or White groups.

Another resolution is to use the concept of *ethnicity* instead of race – particularly when analysing educational opportunity and experiences. Ethnicity is seen as a more sensitive indicator of difference and diversity. It refers to social and cultural ties such as language, custom and practices. Richardson & Lambert (1986) quote two definitions of an ethnic group. First, by Schermerhorn (1970):

> *... a collectivity within a larger society, having real or putative ancestry, memories of a shared historical past, and a cultural focus on one or more symbolic elements defined as the epitome of their people-hood.*

Second, by Yinger (1981)

> *... a segment of a larger society whose members are thought, by themselves and/or by others, to share a common origin and to share important segments of a common culture, and who, in addition, participate in shared activities in which common origin and culture are significant ingredients.*

(Richardson & Lambert, 1986: 53)

On a wider political scale, the use of the concept of ethnicity has been significant in the 1990s. Events in Europe – for example, Bosnia, Serbia, Croatia and Northern Ireland – have established wide use of the concept and, while it is beyond the scope of this Reader to comment further, it is important to recognise the significance and power of cultural allegiances.

Connected to the concept of ethnicity, is that of *ethnic minority*. The term 'minority' is not always used to describe a *numeric* minority (it can be used to describe a group with little power who may, actually, form a majority in numeric terms). But its use in this context is most often to indicate an ethnic group who compose a minority in numeric terms. The term ethnic minority is useful insofar as it reminds us that we *all* have an ethnic group – a cultural heritage.

Differential access and achievement

Following the discussion of terminology, you will note that the 'descriptors' used in the production of statistical evidence with respect to access and achievement vary in the literature. Being aware of this is a good starting point for any analysis.

The next three readings will help with this. The first extract, from Marsh *et al.* (1996), demonstrates the problems that emerge, for example, in using statistical data. Ian Marsh and his colleagues also go on to provide an analysis of the patterns of differential access and attainment in schools, FE and HE.

Race, social class and gender

'Ethnicity' and 'race' are confusing concepts... In general, too many studies of education and race could be justifiably accused of gross simplification because they have forced individuals into inappropriate, homogenous categories and thus misrepresented the unique nature of our ethnic backgrounds. Despite the wide range of ethnic backgrounds in Britain, educational research has tended to categorize individuals into three main, and largely incomprehensible, groups – 'West Indian', 'Asian' and 'Other'. It is easy to see why this has happened. Sociologists study group

Continued...

---

behaviour and are, by the nature of their subject, obliged to allocate individuals into groups. They are also concerned about inequality in education and make such distinctions in order to identify and measure inequality.

Sociologists have also labelled people as 'Black' or 'White' in order to identify racism in education as being primarily based on skin colour, rather than cultural or ethnic identity. However, this raises the possibility that sociologists themselves could be accused of racism because of their tendency to use the categorization of 'Black' to override any other personal characteristic and to label Black children (and 'West Indian' children in particular) negatively as 'under-achievers'.

Research into race and education is therefore fraught with difficulties, first because of the problem of finding suitable ways of labelling groups, second, because there is a temptation to generalize from small samples, and third, because an emphasis on statistical data often means that qualitative differences in educational experiences are ignored. These reservations help to explain why figures relating to various ethnic groups have been included in official, national statistics on education only since 1990–91.

We are left then with the central question: are educational outcomes most influenced by social class, gender or race?

In view of Britain's history of racial discrimination and prejudice we could reasonably ask whether race affects social class and, if so, whether research that intends to study 'race' is actually studying social class. For example, continuous research into school-leavers for both the Rampton Report (1981) and Swann Report (1985) was carried out in five inner city LEA areas where the educational attainment of *every* ethnic group in the study was lower than the national average.

The reports nevertheless confirmed earlier findings (e.g. Tomlinson, 1980) that the performance of 'West Indian' children at O Level/CSE and A Level was markedly lower than that of 'Asians' and 'Others'. The Swann Committee also found that in the time between its fieldwork (1981–2) and the fieldwork for the Rampton Report (1978–9) the performance of 'West Indian' children had improved but was still lower than that of the other groups (Rampton, 1981; Swann, 1985)...

This obviously leads us to ask whether there were differences in the social class background of 'West Indian', 'Asian' and 'Other' children and some evidence of this was provided in 1986 by Eggleston *et al.* According to these findings 87 per cent of children from 'Afro-Caribbean' backgrounds had fathers who were manual workers, compared to 73 per cent of 'Asian' children and 69 per cent of 'white' children. This might suggest that some children were more disadvantaged by social class but, yet again, we encounter the problem of labelling children. Do 'Afro-Caribbean' and 'West Indian' mean the same thing and are the samples comparable?

In 1985 the first national study (of England and Wales: Drew & Gray, 1989) of the achievements of Black young people found that the performance of 'Afro-Caribbeans'

Continued...

was better than in earlier studies, but still concluded that the results of this group had changed little between 1972 and 1985. However, the study went further by considering the relative influences of race, social class, and gender. Drew & Gray found that social class explained more variation in examination performance than did ethnic group or gender, but the combined effects of social class, gender and race still left the larger part of the variation in performance unexplained. This suggests that other, unknown factors were also significant. What factors, other than social class, gender and race, could be particularly significant influences on educational achievements?

We have seen that girls have moved ahead of boys in their educational achievements and this raises questions about the comparative influences of gender and race. Driver (1980) studied five multiracial schools and found that 'West Indian' girls did better than 'West Indian' boys but that, among 'whites', boys did better than girls. It was also found that in these five schools 'West Indian' children performed better in their 16+ examinations than did 'whites'. This raises the possibility that individual school factors might have a significant influence on educational outcomes.

Further evidence of the academic achievements of Black women can be found when we look at the working age population as a whole. Here we can see that there are marked variations according to ethnic groupings and that the 'Black' population is the only group in which women are better qualified than men...

The achievements of Black women have been established long enough to feed through to statistics covering a wide age range. It is therefore reasonable to ask if there are more developments waiting to make a similar impact, and one possible trend has already been identified. Reid (1993) carried out a study of socio-spatial indices and 16+ examination results in Bradford schools in 1991. From a very complex picture he found that the average score at GCSE of 'Asian' girls' was higher than for 'white' boys. Using some indices, 'Asian' girls' achievements were also higher than those of 'Asian' boys and 'white' girls and boys. This structural approach obviously raises various questions that can be investigated only by interpretative research. For example, Lambart (1976) and Fuller (1980) both studied Black girls in school subcultures.

Sociologists have also taken an interest in the achievements of various racial groups at the top end of education, in further education and higher education. Research during the 1980s seemed to confirm the findings about 'West Indian' under-achievement in schools. Craft & Craft (1983) found that, irrespective of social class, 'West Indians' were under-represented in further and higher education. The Swann Report (1985) found that 1 per cent of 'West Indians', 4 per cent of 'Indians', 4 per cent of 'Asians' and 4 per cent of 'Others' went to university. However, the report also found that a larger percentage of 'Asians' and 'West Indians' took some sort of further education course than was general for the whole population. This finding has been supported by more recent research which seems to strongly contradict earlier negative images of the achievements of 'West Indians' or 'Afro-Caribbeans'. Labour Force Surveys between 1988 and 1990 found that not only have the numbers of young people taking some sort of further education increased, but also 'Afro-Caribbeans' and 'South Asians' have maintained a tendency to be over-represented compared to

Continued...

99

'whites'. If we extend our interest to all age ranges in further education we can see that it is 'whites' who are under-represented in further education...

In 1994 the Policy Studies Institute published its findings about the different rates of entry of ethnic minorities into higher education in 1992. It considered the percentages of successful applicants from various groups and found radical differences in access to universities and polytechnics. When looking only at success in access to universities it was found that 'Chinese' and 'Black African' applicants were over-represented compared to their presence in the population as a whole; 'Black Caribbeans' and 'Bangladeshis' were under-represented compared to their presence in the population as a whole. When looking only at success in access to polytechnics it was found that 'Black Caribbeans' were over-represented compared to their presence in the population as a whole. However, the Policy Studies Institute (1994) indicated that a simplistic cause/effect interpretation based on racial categorization is to be avoided; for example a larger proportion of 'Black Caribbeans' applied for access to highly competitive courses (such as medicine and law) and to courses in a relatively small number of universities near to their homes. This meant that competition for places was not evenly spread. The socio-economic inequalities highlighted in the study fell disproportionately on certain ethnic minority groups.

Analysis based only on statistical data is very limited. To achieve any sort of depth of understanding we must also apply an interpretive approach. For example, it is reasonable to ask whether language problems might inhibit the achievements of some children. Many children of 'Asian' origin appear to have thrived in education despite the fact that many of them have English as their second language; in comparison, earlier claims that 'West Indians' were under-achieving seemed peculiar when so many of them had been raised with English as their first language...

Political perspectives on race and racism tend to encompass all of the approaches we have already encountered, ranging from egalitarianism to biological determination and including debates about uniformity, diversity, integration and segregation. Some right-wing perspectives take a 'colour-blind' approach, assuming that children from a wide range of backgrounds will be incorporated into the existing British 'culture', submerging their own cultural heritage in the process. A New Right emphasis accepts individual diversity but assumes that social cohesion can be maintained and promoted by the sound operation of market forces, without government intervention. However, the most extreme right-wing approach is obviously in favour of negative racial discrimination and enforced segregation of some sort.

Centre-ground and left-wing perspectives tend to involve more concern about racism and the negative effects of racial inequalities, but vary in their proposed solutions. A multicultural approach tends to assume that, if children can learn about cultures other than their own, a greater degree of tolerance will be cultivated, not only in the individual, but also in society as a whole. This approach has been criticized for being naive in its understanding of the true nature of racism (caricatured as just being about 'saris and samosas'). It ignores the fact that many children who are born to indigenous 'British' families and in a British 'culture' (if that could be defined) suffer

Continued...

from covert or overt racism simply because they have black or brown skin. Anti-racists therefore argue that it is racism, rather than cultural diversity, that must be confronted. The role of education is to challenge racism in society as a whole by, for example, providing children with positive images of 'Blackness' (Bryan *et al.* 1987). However, a third (and there are probably more) approach tries to assimilate multicultural and anti-racist approaches. Interculturalism promotes a recognition and acceptance of the uniqueness of the individual and the superficiality of labelling anyone simply by, skin colour, 'culture', social class, gender, disability, and so on.

It seems that, despite the problems involved in studying race and education, racism must be acknowledged as a fundamental problem and the role of education in the transmission or amelioration of racism must be considered. Studies of racism in schools are still beset with difficulties due to its often covert nature. There are however, many 'victim reports' of the sort furnished by Bryan *et al.* (1987) and other studies into the nature of racist bullying and name-calling (e.g. Cohen, 1988)... There seem to be no easy answers to our earlier question of whether educational outcomes are most influenced by social class, gender or race.

We can identify some themes and trends at a structural level, and can see some patterns emerging in small-scale interactions, but must still acknowledge education as a unique experience. Race, social class and gender must be recognized as sources of educational inequalities, but their effects and interrelationships must not be distorted by oversimplification. Even the improved educational performance of girls and women does not provide a regular pattern of educational achievement and more equal opportunities. For example, the Policy Studies Institute (1994) found that in 1992 (holding all other variables constant) women were still significantly less likely to be admitted to universities than men.

We have already briefly considered some educational policy options related to social class, gender and race as separate issues – but what can we learn if we compare policies regarding all three? As an acknowledgement of constantly changing education policies and transformations in the achievements of some social groupings we end with more questions, rather than answers. Develop your own theories!

References

Bryan B, Dadzie S & Scafe S (1987) 'Learning to resist: black women and education' in G Werner & M Arnot (eds) *Gender under scrutiny* Hutchinson

Cohen T (1988) 'Sambo: a study in name calling' in E Kelly & T Cohen *Racism in schools: new research evidence* Trentham

Craft M & Craft A (1983) 'The participation of ethnic minority students in further and higher education' *Education Review* 25 (1)

Drew D & Gray J (1989) *The fifth year exam achievements of black young people in England and Wales* University of Sheffield Research Centre

Driver G (1980) 'How West Indians do better in school' *New Society* 17th January

Eggleston J, Dunn D & Anjali M (1986) *Education for some: the educational and vocational experiences of 15–18 year-old members of minority ethnic groups* Trentham

Continued...

101

Fuller M (1980) 'Black girls in a London comprehensive' in R Deem (ed) *Schooling for women's work* Routledge & Kegan Paul

Lambart A (1976) 'The sisterhood' in M Hammersley & P Woods (eds) *Process of schooling* Routledge & Kegan Paul

Policy Studies Institute (1994) *Ethnic minorities and higher education: why are there different rates of entry?* PSI

Rampton Report (1981) *West Indian children in our schools* HMSO

Reid I (1993) 'More than a touch of class' in CESE *The Education Reform Act and equal opportunities: emerging patterns* CESE Conference, Manchester November 1992

Swann Report (1985) *Education for all* HMSO

Tomlinson S (1980) *Educational subnormality: a study in decision making* Routledge

(Marsh *et al.* 1996: 464–470)

Utilising the concept of ethnicity, the following article by Jane Clarke (1997) gives an account of the educational achievements of South Asian young people.

Achievement of South Asian students

As Verma (1989) notes, continued underachievement of ethnic minorities during the 1960s and 1970s prompted the government to investigate the issue through the establishment of the Swann Committee (1985). In their final report, *Education for All*, they found that African-Caribbean children were clearly underachieving, but failed to find any underachievement on the part of South Asians. However, the authors conceded that this may have been due to a lack of standardised school statistics. Indeed, many large-scale projects carried out before the publication of the report had suggested underachievement amongst South Asian communities too.

Achievement levels

The Swann Committee found that South Asian students were more likely to repeat years before gaining O-levels or CSEs, and this has been supported by more recent research (for instance, Tanna, 1990; Taylor, 1993). Swann compared achievement levels of South Asian children with white working-class children and found that Indian students generally achieved at a higher level, whilst concern was expressed about the underperformance of Bangladeshi students. Swann indicated that South Asian children from all social classes underachieved compared with the white middle-class children, a pattern which continues today. What explanations can be given for the continued underachievement of so many of the ethnic minorities represented in Britain? This article will concentrate on South Asian pupils as this demonstrates the complexity of trying to establish the causes of lower academic achievement.

Before looking at possible explanations, it is necessary to clarify which communities were referred to as 'Asian' in Swann. Table 1 shows the diversity of South Asian communities represented in Britain; a variety of languages and religions are represented as well as urban/rural communities.

Continued...

Country	Region	Religions	Languages
Pakistan	Afghanistan Border	Islam	Pushtu
	Mirpur	Islam	Mirpuri/Punjabi
	West Punjab	Islam	Punjabi/Urdu
India	East Punjab	Sikhism	Punjabi
		Hinduism	Hindi/Urdu
	Gujarat	Hinduism	Gujarati
		Islam	Hindi/Urdu
Bangladesh	Sylhet	Islam	Sylheti/Bengali
	Central and Maritime East India	Islam	Bengali

Table 1 Major areas of South Asian emigration with religion and language data

Unfortunately, as Tomlinson (1983) notes in her review of the literature, there are very few large-scale studies which take into account the effects of religious beliefs or first language. Eggleston *et al.* (1986) provided religious and linguistic data but did not carry out any further analysis on it. Others have suggested that such factors could be crucial in understanding underachievement.

Country of origin

Research since Swann has mainly focused on country of origin, and a study involving some 17,000 students in London (Kysel, 1988) showed that both Indian and Pakistani pupils performed better than white working-class students, whereas Bangladeshi pupils were still underachieving: something which the Swann Report had hinted at in its findings. Furthermore, both Modood (1993) and Modood & Shiner (1994) have shown how Indian and Pakistani students are over-represented in higher education applications, whereas applicants by Bangladeshis are lower than expected.

An additional complicating factor is that the Punjabi and Gujarati communities came via the East African (EA) colonies of Kenya, Tanzania and Uganda, whereas the others came directly from the Indian subcontinent. Ballard & Vellins (1985) have demonstrated how EA Asians form a much larger proportion of undergraduate applicants than their representation in Britain would predict. Kysel (1988) discovered that EA Asians came second only after Indians in terms of examination results. Hahlo (1980) suggests that EA Asians had greater opportunities to raise their socio-economic status before coming to Britain, and therefore may have adopted more middle-class views of education. It is also claimed that EA Asians have had greater exposure to the English language, in particular when compared to South Asians from rural communities.

Educationists in general and Tomlinson (1983) in particular have argued that longer exposure to the British educational system should lead to higher achievement

Continued...

amongst South Asian pupils. Findings in Jones (1993) showed how Indian and Pakistani immigration began much earlier than that of the Bangladeshis, whose rate of arrival is still on the increase. This may explain why Bangladeshis are underachieving so noticeably.

Education level of parents

Researchers have also demonstrated how the education level of parents affects the performance of their children. For instance, both South Asian and white children whose parents had no qualifications performed significantly worse in reading and intelligence tests. Indeed, Jones (1993) found that for the age group 25 to 44, which arguably covers most parents with teenage children (as well as others), 31% of Indians had completed their education to A levels or beyond, compared with only 14% of Pakistanis and 12% of Bangladeshis (almost three-quarters of Bangladeshi parents had no qualifications). One possible explanation for South Asians' higher achievement levels amongst ethnic minorities is the value in terms of prestige that they place on education. Gibson & Bhachu (1986) suggest that within the Sikh community education replaces class or caste as a measure of a person's status, claiming that 'for many British Sikhs being a bad student is tantamount to being a failure as a social being' (p33). In contrast, Eggleston found that South Asian parents were less likely than white or African-Caribbean parents to have had any contact with their children's teachers. However, Punjabi teachers suggest that this may be due to working patterns and difficulties with English rather than a lack of interest. Researchers found that amongst Mirpuri families most fathers had visited their child's school.

The value of qualifications

There is evidence of dissatisfaction amongst South Asian parents about the standard of education in Britain: some Pakistani parents find schools in Britain too informal and it has been reported that the Bhattra Sikh community living in Cardiff 'actually feels its identity and way of life to be threatened by the schools'. Discipline, uniform, diet, physical and religious education have been identified as some of the most contentious issues for South Asian families. Despite these reservations, research has shown that South Asians value paper qualifications, seeing them as a form of security. In support of this, Ballard & Vellins (1985) also discovered that South Asian students were more likely than white students to apply to read medicine and less likely to apply to read for arts degrees. Clearly, there are no simple explanations for the lower performance of South Asians and research is still needed to assess the importance of each of the factors above in influencing academic underachievement.

References

Ballard R & Vellins S (1985) 'South Asian entrants to British universities: a comparative note' *New Community* 12 (2), pp260–265

Eggleston J *et al.* (1986) *Education for some: the educational and vocational experiences of 15–18 year-old members of minority ethnic groups* Trentham

Gibson MA & Bhachu P (1986) 'Community forces and school performance: Punjabi Sikhs in rural California and urban Britain' *New Community* 13 (1), pp27–39

Continued...

Hahlo KG (1980) 'Profile of a Gujerati community in Bolton' *New Community* 8 (3), pp295–307

Jones T (1993) *Britain's ethnic minorities* Policy Studies Institute

Kysel F (1988) 'Ethnic background and examination results' *Education Research* 30 (2), pp83–89

Modood T (1993) 'The number of ethnic minority students in British higher education: some grounds for optimism' *Oxford Review of Education* 19 (2), pp167–182

Modood T & Shiner M (1994) *Ethnic minorities and higher education* Policy Studies Institute

Swann Committee (1985) *Education for all: the report for the Committee of Inquiry into the education of children from ethnic minority groups* HMSO

Tanna K (1990) 'Excellence, equality and educational reform: the myth of South Asian achievement levels' *New Community* 16 (3), pp349–368

Taylor P (1993) 'Access to HE: an uneven path?' in H Golbourne & P Lewis-Meeks *Access of ethnic minorities to higher education at Kings College Cambridge* Coventry Centre for Research into Ethnic Relations

Tomlinson S (1983) 'The educational performance of children of Asian origin' *New Community* 10 (3), pp206–212

Verma G (1989) *Education for all: a landmark in pluralism* Falmer Press

(Clarke, 1997: 32–33)

The third of the extracts gives an account of the experiences of a group of black young people of Afro-Caribbean and Asian parentage, as presented by Máirtín Mac an Ghaill (1989).

Racism and education

Casement Sixth Form College is an open-access, co-educational institution, situated in a large industrial Midlands city, in a working-class residential area. It provides courses leading to GCSE, GCE A level and more recently vocational and pre-vocational courses, in response to local labour market changes. In the local area, there has been a decline in the manufacturing sector from 303,000 in 1971 to 159,000 employees in 1987 (Tomkins, 1988). It has a good reputation for academic achievement, with students travelling to it from all over the city. Despite falling rolls within the local education authority, the college has maintained its student numbers at about 500. At the time of the research, there were slightly more males than females. About 12 per cent of the students were of Afro-Caribbean parentage and about 25 per cent were of Asian parentage. It has a male majority teaching staff. Much of the material presented here was collected from observation, informal conversations with the twenty-five students, their secondary school and Casement College teachers, and from recorded semi-structured interviews. In addition, they kept diaries and questionnaires were given to them and a further group of twenty-five black students (see Burgess, 1988). The latter data are not reported here but they informed the carrying out of the study. Also, interviews were carried out with the students' parents and black community representatives.

Continued...

Schooling in multiracist Britain

Black working-class youths in Britain have grown up in a racially stratified society, in which there is little contact between the black and white populations. In interviews, many of the students pointed out that they did not have white friends outside of college and knew few other white people. Their contact with whites tended to be limited to interaction with those who had power over them, such as teachers, career officers and employers. To varying degrees, the students spoke of the pervasiveness of white racism in relation to, *inter alia,* British immigration laws, the housing and labour markets, welfare institutions, policing and media presentation (Home Office, 1981; CRE, 1988). They described their experience of a multiracist society (Cohen & Bains, 1986).

Shazia: Of course, you meet racism all the time. Like if you are walking up the road, racists abuse you. If you're in a queue and there's a lot of you and there's a hold up, the whites will abuse and push past you. What can you do? If you try anything you have a mob against you.

Stephen: In this society you are a black, an immigrant or their ethnic minorities, even though you are born here. That's your prescribed status. These labels are used to divide up the population. They influence where we live, what schools we go to and where we work.

Tahir: I think you can compare being Asian to being a woman in how this society treats both of them. For a woman, it's not that every man is going to rape her but you never know which one. It's the same for Asians and blacks, you have to live with never being able to predict how whites will behave. You must be prepared for potential danger and a lot of them are schizophrenic, like teachers. First OK, then suddenly they change for no reason.

Maxine: At least with the National Front and British Movement you can be prepared, with other whites you just can't tell. They have the power.

Imran: I don't agree with the idea all whites are racists. There's good and bad in every 'race'. I have met good people, whites, who have helped me out.

There was disagreement among the students about the degree to which their secondary schools were racially structured. This disagreement extended to their perception of Casement College. Some of the students, who primarily focused on teacher-student interaction, maintained that they experienced little personal racial antagonism. For others, who took a wider view, including institutional structures and processes, their schools, as part of the wider society, were seen as significant institutions in reproducing racial exclusiveness. What was particularly salient here was that whatever place on the continuum of student awareness of racist schooling they occupied, there was no pre-determined outcome in terms of student responses. It did not directly lead to the taking on of an anti-school or pro-school identity that might lead to academic success or failure. All these students have succeeded within the school system.

Continued...

Helen: I did not seem to have the conscious feeling of racism in the education system that I have succeeded in. Restrictions were never enforced by those teachers, who thought, 'Oh no! This is not a predominant black subject or female subject'. Maybe I looked through rose-coloured glasses and pushed the racism to the back of my mind.

Gilroy: It's the same for me. I could see hints of racism towards certain people but it seemed to be because they weren't working. Of course that was still wrong but it seemed to me that if you worked then you got on OK. Maybe that's how we got through. I think that if you see the racism more clearly at this stage then it's more difficult to get through or at least if you openly fight it, it is.

Laverne: I never got the verbal reasoning cup, I always got the sports cup! Every year my name was called out. It was the racism and I fought it as best I could with my mates.

Kussar: I think the same. I saw a lot of racists. In everyday things the Asian and black kids were seen by teachers as worse and treated differently to whites. But I think that makes you more determined to succeed 'It did me and my friends. We got together and talked this through.

Iftikhar: The whole education system is racist. In fact I think it's probably the most important influence on black people. You can look at how there are no blacks in textbooks and library books. History is from a narrow English or European perspective. Black kids are put into the lowest classes. Our language, our culture is excluded. The teachers have no respect for us. This all happened at our school and it happens in all schools in this society. They are preparing us for the worst jobs.

There was a tendency for students, such as Kussar and Iftikhar, who saw racism within schools not as an aberration of a meritocratic system but as linked to wider socio-economic forces, to ratify the racially structured processes in an overtly functionalist way. What is lacking in such deterministic accounts is the sense of students and teachers, as active agents inside classrooms creating social reality, albeit within specific historical, socio-economic conditions (Dale, 1982). As Kessler *et al.* (1985) maintain, in relation to theorizing gender relations in secondary schooling:

We must find ways of talking about large-scale structures without reifying them and about personal practices without losing their large-scale contexts.

The question of how different black students perceived and responded to schooling became the main focus of my study. The dominant sociological conception of student responses in terms of the dichotomous anti-school/pro-school orientations is inadequate, given the range of black student responses that are examined here. Social reality is more complex than the conventional student typologies suggest, which implicitly adopt a passive conception of socialization that is overly deterministic. A more useful definition is provided by Lacey (1977), who sees it as 'the adoption or creation of appropriate strategies'.

Continued...

107

References

Burgess RG (1988) 'Examining classroom practice using diaries and diary interviews' in P Woods & A Pollard (eds) *Education, society and teaching: a new challenge for the sociology of education* Croom Helm

Cohen P & Baines H (eds) (1986) *Multi-racist Britain* Hutchinson

CRE (1988) *Learning in terror: a survey of racial harassment in schools and colleges* Campaign for Racial Equality

Dale R (1982) 'Education and the capitalist state: contributions and contradictions' in MW Apple (ed) *Cultural and economic reproduction in education* Routledge

Home Office (1981) *Racial attacks* HMSO

Kessler S, Ashenden DJ, Conell RW & Dowsett GW (1985) 'Gender relations in secondary school' *Sociology of Education* 58, pp34–48

Lacey C (1977) *The socialization of teachers* Methuen

Tomkins R (1988) 'A different industrial base' *Financial Times* Section 3 ii 1st Dec.

(Mac an Ghaill, 1989: 274–278)

Disability and differential access and achievement

Much thinking about disability and access gets locked into discussions of physical barriers and looks for answers in the restructuring of the built environment. Whilst this is a central consideration, it should not cloud our understandings of the extent to which people with learning difficulties and disabilities have to struggle for the right in the wider sense to gain access to and participate in programmes of education and training.

Tim Davies, in the next extract, wonders why mainstream sociology seems to pay so little attention to issues of disability; it is generally believed, perhaps, that it is a medical rather than a social matter. He considers in some detail social attitudes towards disabled people and asks how far they are reinforced by representations of disability in the printed and the broadcast media and what role language plays in the reinforcing of stereotypes.

Disabled by society?

Look up 'disability' in the index of any of the standard A level sociology textbooks and you won't find it. Hardly surprising, you might say. What has disability got to do with society? Surely it's a medical matter, or at least an individual one? One that psychology could shed some light on perhaps? But sociology ...?

This article will argue that contrary to such assumptions there is indeed an important social dimension to disability, and that in fact considerable progress has already been made in elucidating this dimension. My intention is to provide an introduction to some of this important work and in doing so demonstrate something of sociology's potential to illuminate the connection between what Wright-Mills (1959) called 'the personal troubles of milieux' and 'the public issues of social structure'.

Continued...

Why so little sociological attention?

The lack of attention paid to disability in A level textbooks is replicated throughout sociology (Jenkins, 1991). Why is this? One seemingly plausible reason is that disabled people are only a small minority of the population and have, therefore, like other minorities before them, simply escaped sociological notice. However, there are at least two problems with this explanation. Firstly, research suggests that disabled people are not such a small minority. The most recent official estimate from the Office of Population Censuses and Surveys (Martin *et al.* 1988) puts the number of disabled adults (16 years and above) in Great Britain at six and a quarter million, or 14% of the population, which is significantly higher, for example, than Great Britain's ethnic minority population – estimated at 4.8%.

These figures cannot of course be accepted uncritically, any more than any other official statistics. And indeed, they have been challenged both by those who say they represent an underestimate (e.g. Hirst, 1989) and by those who argue that they are an overestimate (e.g. the Minister for the Disabled responding to the publication of these figures). But whatever the 'true' numbers, the second problem with this explanation is that sociological interest in any case is not simply a matter of numbers. Small numbers have not prevented considerable sociological interest in, for example, religious sects, professional criminals and suicide victims; and large numbers did not prevent women from being largely ignored by sociologists until recent decades.

If it is not a matter of numbers, then, what is the explanation? Answers to this question must necessarily be speculative, but I would suggest that there are at least three reasons.

- Firstly, it is probable that few sociologists are themselves disabled. This is not a situation specific to sociology, but a reflection of the employment problems faced by disabled people which has resulted in a situation in which for example only 12% of the disabled workforce hold professional or managerial positions compared with 21% of the non-disabled workforce (Barnes, 1991).

- Secondly, disability typically provokes complex emotional responses in the non-disabled: a mixture of guilt, fear, anxiety, pity and embarrassment. The easiest way of dealing with such painful feelings is through avoidance, which in this case means not studying disability.

- However, almost certainly the most important reason has to do with the whole way in which disability has been understood in the past, namely, as an individual and specifically a *medical* problem rather than as a social issue.

The medical model

From the 'medical model' perspective disabled people are seen as being in need of care by medical personnel – doctors and nurses. The medical model is an example of what social scientists call an 'individualistic' approach to understanding society. Such approaches explain features of society by reference to the characteristics of the individuals involved. But in doing so they ignore wider social influences which impinge upon the individual and which may be largely outside the individual's control.

Continued...

It is this limitation of the medical model which has been recognised and increasingly challenged in recent years by an alternative perspective on disability known as the 'social model'. This model changes the focus from the individual disabled person to the society in which he or she is located. However, to understand what this model is saying we must first look more closely at the nature of disability and the terms that describe it.

Defining disability

In talking about disability, three terms constantly recur in the literature: impairment, disability itself, and handicap. These terms are often used interchangeably, but to understand the social model it is vital to distinguish between them. A starting point is offered by the definitions used by the World Health Organisation. 'Impairment' refers to 'any loss or abnormality of psychological, physiological or anatomical structure or function'. 'Disability' refers to the resulting difficulties in performing 'normal' activities and 'handicap' is the resulting disadvantage experienced by people with impairments in performing 'normal' roles. Thus, for example, some may have a hearing impairment which means they have difficulty in picking up conversation ('disabled') and as a result are disadvantaged when it comes to taking part in face-to-face social interaction ('handicapped'). This sounds logical enough, albeit somewhat complex, but the implication that disability and handicap are determined by impairment has been challenged by supporters of the social model.

One early influential critique was provided by Ann Shearer (1981). She argued that whilst disability 'is something that has to be taken as given', handicap 'is something imposed on that disability to make it more limiting than it must necessarily be'. And it is imposed largely by the patterns and expectations of a society organised by and for the non-disabled. Shearer illustrates this point by arguing that not being able to run for a bus would not be a handicap if buses waited for their passengers! This distinction between disability and handicap is still in widespread use today, but disabled people and their organisations are increasingly unhappy with the use of the word 'handicap' because of its association with 'cap in hand', i.e. begging. Consequently, they have pushed for an end to the use of this term and for the use instead of a simple distinction between impairment and disability. Thus Barnes (1992) suggests that 'impairment' should be used to refer to 'individually based functional limitations – whether physical, intellectual, sensory or hidden' – 'but disability is the loss or limitation of opportunities to take part in the normal life of the community on an equal level with others due to physical and social barriers'.

The social model

We are now in a position to see what a radical challenge to conventional – medically inspired – perceptions of disability the social model represents. It is arguing nothing less than that people with impairments are disabled by society, by the way society's institutions operate and by the attitudes and beliefs non-disabled people hold about disabled people. All of these act as barriers preventing disabled people from participating fully in society.

Continued...

The term 'disableism' has recently been coined to describe these barriers. Thompson (1993) offers a helpful definition of disableism as 'the combination of social forces, cultural values and personal prejudices which marginalises disabled people, portrays them in a negative light and thus oppresses them'. The introduction of another 'ism' (cf. 'sexism', 'racism', 'ageism') may seem trite – as Thompson says – but if we now go on to look at each of these barriers in turn we will see that there is overwhelming evidence for the existence of such an ideology and its associated practices.

The built environment

In a seminal article by Vic Finkelstein (1975) a world is imagined in which wheelchair-users and able-bodied people lead completely segregated lives. The wheelchair-users develop their society to meet their own needs and construct a built environment which reflects the fact that everyone uses a wheelchair. In due course some able-bodied people come to settle in the village. What do you think happens? Yes, you are right. They find themselves constantly knocking their heads on the door lintels and ceilings which were lower since there was no need to build them at a conventional height. Indeed, able-bodied people find themselves 'disabled'. Of course in the world as it is, ablebodied people hold most of the reins of power and the built environment therefore tends to neglect the needs of disabled people creating access problems to shops, offices, cinemas, transport, and so on. However, this is one area where changes have begun to take place. Special government regulations now cover the provision of access for disabled people in the construction of new buildings. Nevertheless, research indicates that there is still a long way to go; Pointon (1992) refers to a recent study by Milner & Urquart which revealed that only 8 out of 38 British schools of architecture have course documentation that specifically refers to the access requirements of disabled people.

Institutional discrimination

Institutional discrimination refers to organisational practices, procedures and policies which, whether intending to or not, treat one group less favourably than another... Research initiated and monitored by the British Council of Organisations of Disabled People (Barnes, 1991) documents the existence of impairment-related discrimination in the areas of education, employment, benefits, health and social support, housing, transport, leisure, social life and politics. For example, in the field of employment, disabled applicants are six times more likely to be turned down for a job than non-disabled applicants and three times more likely to be unemployed. Moreover, an implicit theme of this study is that the situation has worsened since the 1970s rather than improved.

Attitudes and beliefs

Underlying much of this discrimination is a set of negative attitudes and beliefs about disability that are commonplace in our culture:

But the major difficulties which we face are those created by prejudice and discrimination, by the assumption that our lives are not worth living, our exclusion by those who feel we do not belong.

(Morris, 1992)

Continued...

Disabled people tend to be stigmatised, i.e. seen as possessing a characteristic that is socially discrediting. This perception is based in part on stereotypical views of disabled people which are overwhelmingly negative. So, for example, wheelchair-users are stereotyped as ugly, asexual, intellectually impaired, unable to speak for themselves ('Does he take sugar?'), bitter and dependent.

The poem 'Tell Them The Truth' illustrates how people with intellectual impairments are stereotyped. However, it is important to recognise that these negative perceptions are also a product of the imposition of a set of social norms which reflect the preconceptions of non-disabled people. The application of these norms to disabled people leads to their being labelled 'deviant' (McNeill, 1988).

'Tell Them The Truth'

There goes the mongol up the street
Getting on the looneybus
The schoolbairns call
making funny faces at us
Calling us names
Headcase, spassy, wally
Nutter, Dylan, Twit!

There goes the dumb-bell in the nuthoose!
The Schoolbairns are all daft themselves
They should see a psychiatrist
About their brains
It makes you mad, it boils up your blood
Their wooden heads are full of nonsense

They've got nothing else to do
Except make fun of us
We are human beings
And should be treated as equals
Treated as adults
Tell them the truth.

Donald Lack, Robert Drysdale, Margaret Williamson, Derek Mustard, JR Grubb, Joan Cargil, Robert McMahon: St Clair Centre, Kirkcaldy (group poem: dictated).

(Source: Atkinson & Williams, 1990)

Hevey (quoted in Barnes, 1992) suggests that the link between impairment and all that is socially unacceptable was first established in Classical Greek Theatre, but it persists because stereotypical assumptions are reproduced through the various agents of socialisation in society, particularly language and the media. Moreover these stereotypes are extremely powerful. Firstly, because social segregation limits the amount of everyday contact between disabled and non-disabled people which would help to break down these stereotypes. Secondly, because disability acts as a

Continued...

'master status', i.e. disabled people come to be seen purely in terms of their impairment, which is taken as totally defining them. The consequence of this, as Ryan & Thomas (1980) explain, is that disabled people have been seen 'primarily in terms of what is wrong or abnormal about them' rather than in terms of the characteristics they share with non-disabled people. It will be helpful to look at each of these influences in a little more detail.

Language

Clearly, many of the words used about disabled people, as the poem illustrates in the case of intellectual impairment, are intentionally derogatory and abusive. But in considering the role of language as an agent of socialisation we need to go far beyond the narrow – albeit non-trivial – issues raised by such terms. Phrases that might appear quite innocuous are nevertheless charged with meanings that carry negative connotations. For example, the use of phrases like 'the deaf', 'spastics', 'epileptics', 'the blind', etc. is discouraged by disabled people's organisations as they argue that it tends to dehumanise and objectify disabled people.

Such sensitivity to language use – a sensitivity shared incidentally by other minority groups – may seem to be out of all proportion to its importance. After all, isn't it true that 'sticks and stones may break my bones, but words can never harm me'? The short answer has to be 'no'. Language doesn't simply reflect the world; it constructs the world for us by the meanings it conveys. So, in learning a language we learn to see the world in a particular way; if you want to change the way disabled people are often seen you have to challenge the way language is used. As Michael Oliver has put it:

> *Disabled people know only too well that taking control of what they are going to be called is not a triviality. It is much more important than that: it's part of a wider process of empowering ourselves to take control of all aspects of our lives.*

(*The Observer,* 2 September 1990)

Media representations

Research into media representations of disability is as yet fairly limited, but already there is a good deal of evidence that such representations reflect a relatively narrow range of themes. In a wide-ranging survey that looks at books, films, television, radio and the press, Barnes (1992) identifies, among others, the following themes:

- the disabled person as pitiable and pathetic (reinforced by much charity advertising and by the growth of TV charity shows like 'Children in Need' and 'Telethon');
- the disabled person as sinister and evil (from Shakespeare's *Richard III* through to the 'dwarf' in *Twin Peaks);*
- the disabled person as atmosphere or curio (from Frankenstein's 'hunchback' servant to *The Elephant Man);*
- and the disabled person as an object of violence (from the classic *Whatever Happened to Baby Jane* in which Joan Crawford was a wheelchair-user wholly at the mercy of her murderous sister, Bette Davis, to *Wait Until Dark* in which Audrey Hepburn was a blind woman terrorised by a gang of juvenile delinquents).

Continued...

Barnes acknowledges that not all representations are negative – many focus on the 'extraordinary' achievements or 'remarkable' courage of disabled people – on the disabled person as 'super cripple', as he puts it. But even these he argues are stereotypical, tending to reflect non-disabled people's assumptions about what it must be like to have an impairment rather than the lived experience of most disabled people.

As rock legend Ian Dury, who had polio as a child, put it in a radio interview:

People give you credit because you're getting on with your life [but] I've known people who are bald suffer far more than I ever have when the wind blows the flap off the top of their heads.

(*Punters*, BBC Radio 4, July 1991)

Another recent study by Cumberbatch & Negrine (1992) analysed six weeks of prime-time television broadcasts across all channels in 1988. The most striking feature they discovered was the virtual invisibility of disabled people outside news broadcasts and specialist programmes like the BBC's *One in Four* and Channel 4's *Same Difference:* there were no disabled people in any of the current affairs programmes or game shows and they represented just 0.5% of all the characters portrayed in fictional programmes.

The disability movement

The development and promotion of a social model of disability is inextricably bound up with the growth of a civil rights movement amongst disabled people. In this context it is important to distinguish between organisations of and organisations for disabled people.

Traditionally, disabled people have been represented by charitable organisations funded and run by non-disabled people, such as the Spastics Society [Scope], Mencap, RNIB, RNID. Such organisations for disabled people are often seen by many of the organisations of disabled people as problematic since they perpetuate disabled people's dependence on charity. Organisations such as Disabled Peoples International and BCODP (both founded in 1981 by disabled people themselves) argue for 'Rights not Charity' and are highly critical of the fact that disabled people have often not had a voice in the voluntary organisations that are supposed to represent them.

There are clear parallels between the disability movement and the efforts of other minority groups to bring about social change, particularly women, black people, gays and lesbians. Indeed much of the literature produced by organisations of disabled people indicates a conscious identification with the situation of such groups and a recognition of the existence of 'multiple oppressions' experienced by people who belong to more than one of these groups. These movements have already produced far-reaching changes in society and the disability movement in its turn is likely to bring about further significant changes in the 1990s, engaged as it is in what has been called 'the last great civil rights battle'.

Continued...

Disability and sociology

I hope that I have said enough by now to demonstrate that disability, far from falling outside the province of sociology in fact links up with some of the most basic areas of sociological concern: integration and segregation, culture and ideology, power and politics, normality and deviance, social differentiation and social stratification. Theoretical efforts by sociologists to get to grips with these various strands have been proceeding largely unnoticed by mainstream sociology.

Oliver (1990) refers to the work of sociologists from traditions as diverse as functionalism, interactionism, Marxism, and Weberianism and his own book offers an incisive Gramscian-inspired (Marxist) analysis. There can be little justification therefore for the continued marginalisation of disability within mainstream sociology.

References

Atkinson D & Williams F (eds) (1990) *Know me as I am* Hodder & Stoughton
Barnes C (1991) *Disabled people in Britain and discrimination: a case for anti-discrimination legislation* Hurst & Co in association with BCODP
Barnes C (1992) *Disabling imagery and the media* BCODP and Ryburn
Cumberbatch G & Negrine R (1992) *Images of disability on television* Routledge
Finkelstein V (1975) 'To deny or not to deny disability' reprinted in A Brechin *et al.* (eds) (1981) *Handicap in a social world* Hodder & Stoughton
Hirst M (1989) 'Time to tip the scale' *Insight* 31st January
Jenkins R (1991) 'Disability and social stratification' *British Journal of Sociology* 42 (4)
Martin J, Meltzer H & Elliot D (1988) 'The prevalence of disability amongst adults' *OPCS Surveys of Disability in Great Britain* HMSO
McNeill P (1988) 'Handicapping the disabled' *New Statesman and Society* 10th April
Morris J (1992) *Disabled lives: many voices, one message* BBC Education
Oliver M (1990) *The politics of disablement* Macmillan
Pointon A (1992) 'Access and the architect' in *Disabling world* Channel 4 Television
Ryan J & Thomas F (1980) *The politics of mental handicap* Penguin
Shearer A (1981) *Disability: whose handicap?* Blackwell
Thompson (1993) [no reference given]
Wright-Mills C (1959) *The sociological imagination* Oxford University Press

(Davies, 1994: 15–19)

Our final extract is from the University of Greenwich booklet (1998) *Access to Learning for Students with Disabilities*. It illustrates one way in which an institution can attempt to address the issues that Davies has been discussing.

Disability awareness raising

Traditional views of disability are firmly entrenched and still dominate current thinking. Disability is seen as a personal tragedy (Oliver 1990) and responses to it are largely individualised and inspired by philanthropic notions. In educational

Continued...

terms, the provision of access, or the integration of disabled students, has been concerned with normalisation, i.e. assisting and supporting the student to fit into existing structures with the minimum of modification. Provision has, in the old model, involved a focus on remediation, extra support, withdrawal groups, and extra technological aids. It compensates for disability, and tries to eliminate differences.

This model of support is rooted in a view of disability as a deficit, an approach which many, including disabled people themselves, have begun to criticise as failing to address the issue of genuine access to an equal opportunity and as perpetuating discriminatory practices by perpetuating the status quo in education (Oliver, 1990; Barnes, 1991). Currently a different model is being proposed, whereby genuine access to learning for disabled students is planned within an inclusive framework. This provision will recognise difference and diversity as enriching and will begin to offer access for all to the full curriculum. All our learning and teaching approaches should support this aim. The result will be a celebration of difference.

Perhaps the most important issues here are concerned with the way in which we as education providers, lecturers, support staff, and Student Services, approach the difference amongst our students. Unless we underpin all our work with a clear understanding of the equal opportunities messages defined in the model above we are in danger of being responsible for creating barriers inhibiting access to learning and of perpetuating discriminatory practice which will seriously disadvantage disabled students.

References

Barnes C (1991) *Disabled people in Britain and discrimination: a case for anti-discrimination legislation* Hurst & Co in association with BCODP
Oliver M (1990) *The politics of disablement* Macmillan

(Lloyd, 1998: 5)

References

Abbott P & Wallace C (1997) *An introduction to sociology: feminist perspectives* 2nd edn Routledge
Bates I (1993) 'When I have my own studio...' in I Bates & G Riseborough *Youth and inequality* Oxford University Press
Bilton T (1996) 'Cultural deprivation' in T Bilton *et al. Introductory sociology* 3rd edn Macmillan
Bilton T *et al.* (1996) *Introductory sociology* 3rd edn Macmillan
Clarke J (1997) 'Ethnicity and education revisited' *Sociology Review* 7 (2) November
Davies T (1994) 'Disabled by society?' *Sociology Review* 4 (4) April
Giddens A (1997) *Sociology* 3rd edn Polity Press
Jones C & Mahony P (eds) (1989) *Learning our lines: sexuality and social control in education* Women's Press
Kelly L (1992) 'Not in front of the children' in M Arnot & L Barton *Voicing concerns: sociological perspectives on contemporary educational reforms* Triangle

Lloyd C (1998) *Access to learning for students with disabilities* University of Greenwich

Mac an Ghaill M (1989) 'Coming of age in 1980s England' *British Journal of Sociology of Education* 10 (3)

Marsh I *et al.* (eds) (1996) *Making sense of society: an introduction to sociology* Longman

Reid I (1996) 'Education and inequality' *Sociology Review* 6 (2) November

Richardson J & Lambert J (1986) *The sociology of race* Causeway Press Ltd

Part Three – Maintaining an Effective Learning Environment

We all have memories of teachers we regarded as being highly effective. Their lessons were interesting and enjoyable yet they always seemed to be in control of the class and could silence misbehaviour with a glance. In essence they were able to motivate their students and while doing so they exhibited effective classroom management skills. The final Part of the Reader is concerned with how teachers can go about establishing and maintaining learning conditions such as these.

Teachers are responsible for ensuring that they create an environment which fulfils the following two conditions:

- Firstly it should be one in which students and trainees are able to feel committed to, and interested in, the course or training programme they are following.

The first contribution to Part Three is from a chapter by Robert Biehler and Jack Snowman in which they analyse three theoretical and psychological approaches to motivation – behavioural, cognitive and humanistic. They provide detailed insights into how teachers can apply these to the classroom context and thus motivate the individuals in their classes.

- Secondly it should be a well-managed environment and one which is conducive to learning.

In the final extract Biehler & Snowman consider issues of classroom management. They survey some of the theoretical research into those management and leadership styles which help to identify and analyse the classroom management techniques of effective teachers. By emphasising strategies for the prevention of behavioural problems, they provide useful practical advice for all teachers and trainers.

Though the research which Biehler & Snowman review is largely American, and the institutional context the American high school, there is nothing in these two chapters which is not directly applicable to the post-16 sector of education and training in the United Kingdom. The extracts bring us firmly back to a consideration of attitudes, and thus to some of the issues that we discussed in Part One of this Reader.

7.   Motivation

Robert Biehler & Jack Snowman

Motivation is typically defined as 'the forces that account for the arousal, selection, direction, and continuation of behavior'. Nevertheless, many teachers have at least two major misconceptions about motivation that prevent them from using this concept with maximum effectiveness. One misconception is that some students are unmotivated. Strictly speaking, that is not an accurate statement. As long as a student chooses goals and expends a certain amount of effort to achieve them, he is, by definition, motivated. What teachers really mean is that students are not motivated to behave in the way teachers would like them to behave. The second misconception is that one person can directly motivate another. This view is inaccurate because motivation comes from within a person. What you *can* do, with the help of the various motivation theories discussed in this chapter, is create the circumstances that *influence* students to do what you want them to do.

Many factors determine whether the students in your classes will be motivated or not motivated to learn. You should not be surprised to discover that no single theoretical interpretation of motivation explains all aspects of student interest or lack of it. Different theoretical interpretations do, however, shed light on why some students in a given learning situation are more likely to want to learn than others. Furthermore, each theoretical interpretation can serve as the basis for the development of techniques for motivating students in the classroom. Several theoretical interpretations of motivation ... will now be summarized.

Behavioral views of motivation

Operant conditioning and social learning theory

The effect of reinforcement [BF Skinner and the behaviorists emphasized] the role of reinforcement in learning. After demonstrating that organisms tend to repeat actions that are reinforced and that behavior can be shaped by reinforcement, Skinner developed the technique of programmed instruction to make it possible for students to be reinforced for every correct response. Supplying the correct answer – and being informed by the program that it *is* the correct answer – motivates the student to go on to the next frame; and as the student works through the program, the desired terminal behavior is progressively shaped.

Following Skinner's lead, many behavioral learning theorists devised techniques of behavior modification. Students are motivated to complete a task by being promised a reward of some kind. Many times the reward takes the form of praise or a grade. Sometimes it is a token that can be traded in for some desired object; and at other times the reward may be the privilege of engaging in a self-selected activity.

Operant conditioning interpretations of learning help reveal why some students react favorably to particular subjects and dislike others. For instance, some students may

121

enter a required math class with a feeling of delight, while others may feel that they have been sentenced to prison. Skinner suggests that such differences can be traced to past experiences. He would argue that the student who loves math has been shaped to respond that way by a series of positive experiences with math. The math hater, in contrast, may have suffered a series of negative experiences.

The power of persuasive models Social learning theorists, such as Albert Bandura, call attention to the importance of observation, imitation, and vicarious reinforcement (expecting to receive the same reinforcer that we see someone else get for exhibiting a particular behavior). A student who identifies with and admires a teacher of a particular subject may work hard partly to please the admired individual and partly to try becoming like that individual. A student who observes an older brother or sister reaping benefits from earning high grades may strive to do the same with the expectation of experiencing the same or similar benefits. A student who notices that a classmate receives praise from the teacher after acting in a certain way may decide to imitate such behavior to win similar rewards... Both vicarious reinforcement and direct reinforcement can raise an individual's sense of self-efficacy for a particular task, which, in turn, leads to higher levels of motivation.

Limitations of the behavioral view

While approaches to motivation based on positive reinforcement are often useful, you should be aware of the disadvantages that can come from overuse or misuse of such techniques. Most of the criticisms of the use of reinforcement as a motivational incentive stem from the fact that it represents *extrinsic motivation*. That is, the learner decides to engage in an activity (such as participate in class, do homework, study for exams) to earn a reward that is not inherently related to the activity (such as receive praise from the teacher, earn a high grade, or enjoy the privilege of doing something different). By contrast, students under the influence of *intrinsic motivation* study a subject or acquire a skill because it produces such inherently positive consequences as becoming more knowledgeable, competent, and independent.

Although extrinsic motivation is widespread in society (individuals are motivated to engage in many activities because they hope to win certificates, badges, medals, public recognition, prizes, or admiration from others), this approach has at least three potential dangers. First, changes in behavior may be temporary. As soon as the extrinsic reward has been obtained, the student may revert to such earlier behaviors as studying inconsistently, turning in poor quality homework, and disrupting class with irrelevant comments and behaviors. Second, students may develop a materialistic attitude toward learning. They may think (or say), 'What tangible reward will I get if I agree to learn this information?' If the answer is 'none,' they may decide to make little or no effort to learn it. Third, giving students extrinsic rewards for completing a task may lessen whatever intrinsic motivation they may have for that activity (Kohn, 1993).

This last disadvantage, which is referred to as the *undermining effect,* has been extensively investigated by researchers. It appears that giving students rewards may indeed decrease their intrinsic motivation for a task, but only when (1) initial interest in the activity is very high, (2) the rewards used are not reinforcers (meaning they do not increase the desired behavior), (3) the rewards are held out in advance as incentives, and, most important, (4) the rewards are given simply for engaging in an activity (Cameron & Pierce, 1994; Chance, 1992).

However, there are two instances in which external rewards can enhance intrinsic motivation. First, when rewards are given according to some predetermined standard of excellence, when the task is moderately challenging, and when the reward is relatively large, intrinsic interest in the task is likely to increase. Second, intrinsic motivation can be enhanced when the task is moderately challenging and the size of the reward is consistent with the individual's perceived level of skill. If a student wins first prize in a science fair, for example, and believes that her project was truly superior to those of the other participants, a large reward may cause the student to maintain a strong interest in science (Morgan, 1984).

Why do external rewards undermine intrinsic motivation when they are given just for performing a task? One possible reason is that human beings have an innate drive to be competent (an idea we will discuss in the next section), and rewards that are given irrespective of quality of performance say nothing about an individual's level of competence on moderately difficult tasks. The second possibility is that beginning in early childhood we learn to equate the promise of a reward with the performance of an unpleasant activity. Students may therefore come to believe that 'if somebody promises me a reward to do something, it will probably be unpleasant'. Furthermore, the type of reward seems to make no difference. Tangible rewards (such as toys and candy) and social rewards (such as praise and honors) can be equally effective in undermining or enhancing intrinsic motivation. These results strongly suggest that teachers should avoid the indiscriminate use of rewards for influencing classroom behavior, particularly when an activity seems to be naturally interesting to students. Instead, rewards should be used to provide students with information about their level of competence on tasks they have not yet mastered (Morgan, 1984).

Cognitive views of motivation

Cognitive views stress that human behavior is influenced by the way people think about themselves and their environment. The direction that behavior takes can be explained by four influences: the inherent need to construct an organized and logically consistent knowledge base, one's expectations for successfully completing a task, the factors that one believes account for success and failure, and one's beliefs about the nature of cognitive ability.

The impact of cognitive development

This view is based on Jean Piaget's principles of equilibration, assimilation, accommodation, and schema formation. Piaget proposes that children possess an inherent desire to maintain a sense of organization and balance in their conception of the world (equilibration). A sense of equilibration may be experienced if a child

123

assimilates a new experience by relating it to an existing scheme, or the child may accommodate by modifying an existing scheme if the new experience is too different.

In addition, individuals will repeatedly use new schemes because of an inherent desire to master their environment. This explains why young children can, with no loss of enthusiasm, sing the same song, tell the same story, and play the same game over and over and why they repeatedly open and shut doors to rooms and cupboards with no seeming purpose. It also explains why older children take great delight in collecting and organizing almost everything they can get their hands on and why adolescents who have begun to attain formal operational thinking will argue incessantly about all the unfairness in the world and how it can be eliminated (Stipek, 1993).

The need for achievement

Have you ever decided to take on a moderately difficult task (like take a course on astronomy even though you are a history major and have only a limited background in science) and then found that you had somewhat conflicting feelings about it? On the one hand, you felt eager to start the course, confident that you would be pleased with your performance. But on the other hand, you also felt a bit of anxiety because of the small possibility of failure. Now try to imagine the opposite situation. In reaction to a suggestion to take a course outside your major, you flat out refuse because the probability of failure seems great, while the probability of success seems quite small.

In the early 1960s John Atkinson (1964) proposed that such differences in achievement behavior are due to differences in something called the *need for achievement*. Atkinson described this need as a global, generalized desire to attain goals that require some degree of competence. He saw this need as being partly innate and partly the result of experience. Individuals with a high need for achievement have a stronger expectation of success than they do a fear of failure for most tasks and therefore anticipate a feeling of pride in accomplishment. When given a choice, high-need achievers seek out moderately challenging tasks because they offer an optimal balance between challenge and expected success. By contrast, individuals with a low need for achievement avoid such tasks because their fear of failure greatly outweighs their expectation of success, and they therefore anticipate feelings of shame. When faced with a choice, they typically opt either for relatively easy tasks because the probability of success is high or rather difficult tasks because there is no shame in failing to achieve a lofty goal.

Atkinson's point about taking fear of failure into account in arranging learning experiences has been made more recently by William Glasser in *Control Theory in the Classroom* (1986) and *The Quality School* (1990). Glasser argues that for people to succeed at life in general, they must first experience success in one important aspect of their lives. For most children, that one important part should be school. But the traditional approach to evaluating learning, which emphasizes comparative grading (commonly called 'grading on the curve'), allows only a minority of students to achieve As and Bs and feel successful. The self-worth of the remaining students (who may be quite capable) suffers, which depresses their motivation to achieve on subsequent classroom tasks (Covington, 1985).

Explanations of success and failure: attribution theory

Some interesting aspects of success and failure are revealed when students are asked to explain why they did or did not do well on some task. The four reasons most commonly given stress: ability, effort, task difficulty, and luck. To explain a low score on a math test, for example, different students might make the following statements:

'I just have a poor head for numbers.' (lack of ability)

'I didn't really study for the exam.' (lack of effort)

'That test was the toughest I've ever taken.' (task difficulty)

'I guessed wrong about which sections of the book to study.' (luck)

Because students *attribute* success or failure to the factors just listed, research of this type contributes to what is referred to as *attribution theory*.

Students with long histories of academic failure and a weak need for achievement typically attribute their success to easy questions or luck and their failures to lack of ability. Ability is a stable attribution (that is, people expect its effect on achievement to be pretty much the same from one task to another), while task difficulty and luck are both external attributions (in other words, people feel they have little control over their occurrence). Research has shown that stable attributions, particularly ability, lead to expectations of future success or failure, whereas internal attributions (those under personal control) lead to pride in achievement and reward attractiveness following success or lead to shame following failure. Because low-achieving students attribute failure to low ability, future failure is seen as more likely than future success. In addition, ascribing success to factors beyond one's control diminishes the possibility of taking pride in achievement and placing a high value on rewards. Consequently, satisfactory achievement and reward may have little effect on the failure-avoiding strategies that poor students have developed over the years.

Success-oriented students (high-need achievers), in contrast, typically attribute success to ability and effort and failure to insufficient effort. Consequently, failure does not diminish expectancy of success, feelings of competence, or reward-attractiveness for these students. They simply resolve to work harder in the future (Graham & Weiner, 1993).

Beliefs about the nature of cognitive ability

Throughout the primary and elementary grades, most children believe that academic ability is closely related to effort; if one works hard, one succeeds and becomes 'smarter'. But as these same children reach the middle school and high school grades, many of them adopt a different view. Cognitive ability now comes to be seen as a trait – a fixed, stable part of a person that basically cannot be changed. It is not uncommon, for example, to hear older children and adolescents talk about peers who do or do not have 'it' (Anderman & Maehr, 1994). Why this change occurs, and why it occurs in some individuals but not others, is not entirely known, but the increased emphasis on norm-referenced grading procedures ... is suspected of playing a major role. One casualty of this belief is motivation for learning.

Carol Dweck, who has done extensive research on this topic (see, for example, Cain & Dweck, 1995; Henderson & Dweck, 1990), has found that students can be placed into one of two categories based on their beliefs about the nature of cognitive ability.

On the one hand are students who subscribe to what Dweck calls an *entity theory* because they talk about intelligence (another term for cognitive ability) as if it were a thing or an entity that has fixed characteristics. On the other hand are students who believe that intelligence can be improved through the use of new thinking skills. Dweck describes these students as subscribing to an *incremental theory* to reflect their belief that intelligence can be gradually improved by degrees or increments.

Students who believe that intelligence is an unchangeable thing are primarily motivated to prove their ability by getting high grades and praise and by avoiding low grades and criticism. They report feeling bright or capable when they do not make major mistakes on a test or assignment or when they are among the first students to turn in a paper. If their confidence in their ability is low, they are likely to avoid challenging tasks. If avoidance is not possible, they become discouraged at the first sign of difficulty. This, in turn, produces anxiety, ineffective problem solving, and withdrawal from the task (as a way to avoid concluding that one lacks ability and thereby maintain some self-esteem). According to attribution theory, entity theorists should continue this pattern since success is not attributed to effort, but failure is attributed to low ability.

Those who believe that intelligence is a fixed trait and who are highly confident of their ability are likely to demonstrate such mastery-oriented behaviors as seeking challenges and persisting in the face of difficulty. Both high-confidence and low-confidence entity theorists strive to achieve high grades in order to be praised for their brightness. When confronted with a new task, their initial thought is likely to be 'Am I smart enough to do this?' They may forgo opportunities to learn new ideas and skills if they think they will become confused and make mistakes.

Students with incremental beliefs tend to be motivated to acquire new and more effective cognitive skills. They seek challenging tasks and do not give up easily because they see obstacles as a natural part of the learning process. They often tell themselves what adults have told them for years – 'Think carefully,' 'Pay attention,' and 'Try to recall useful information that was learned earlier.' They seem to focus on the questions 'How do you do this?' and 'What can I learn from this?' Errors are seen as opportunities for useful feedback.

Limitations of cognitive views

Cognitive development. While cognitive development theory can be useful as a means for motivating students, it has a major limitation: it is not always easy or even possible to induce students to experience a cognitive disequilibrium sufficient to stimulate them to seek answers. This is particularly true if an answer can be found only after comparatively dull and unrewarding information and skills are mastered. (How many elementary school students, for example, might be expected to experience a self-impelled urge to learn English grammar or to acquire skill in mathematics?) You are likely to gain some firsthand experience with the difficulty of arousing cognitive disequilibrium the first time you ask students to respond to what you hope will be a provocative question for class discussion. Some students may experience a feeling of intellectual curiosity and be eager to clarify their thinking, but others may stare out the window or do homework for another class.

Need for achievement. Perhaps the major problem that teachers have in using Atkinson's theory of need for achievement is the lack of efficient and objective instruments for measuring its strength. Although you could probably draw reasonably accurate conclusions about whether a student has a high or low need for achievement by watching that student's behavior over time and in a variety of situations, you may not be in a position to make extensive observations. And the problem with short-term observations is that a student's achievement orientation may be affected by more or less chance circumstances. A student might do well on a first exam in a course, for example, because the teacher gave in-class time for study and happened to offer advice at a crucial point during the study period. The high score on that test might inspire the student to work for an A in that class. But if that exam happened to be scheduled the day after a two week bout with the flu, the student might not be well prepared and could end up with a C or D grade. Such a poor performance might cause the student to forget about the A and concentrate instead on obtaining a C.

Attribution theory and beliefs about ability. The major implication of the idea that faulty attributions are at least partly responsible for sabotaging students' motivation for learning is to teach students to make more appropriate attributions. But this is likely to be a substantial undertaking requiring a concerted, co-ordinated effort. One part of the problem in working with students who attribute failure to lack of ability is that ability tends to be seen as a stable factor that is relatively impervious to change. The other part of the problem is that the same students often attribute their success to task difficulty and luck, two factors that cannot be predicted or controlled because they are external and random. Ideas about how to teach students to make more appropriate attributions for success and failure can be found in *Enhancing Motivation: Change in the Classroom* (1976), by Richard deCharms. An additional limitation is that attribution training is not likely to be fully effective with elementary school children. For them, two individuals who learn the same amount of material are equally smart despite the fact that one person has to work twice as long to achieve that goal.

Older children and adolescents, however, have a better grasp of the concept of efficiency; they see ability as something that influences the amount and effectiveness of effort (Stipek, 1993).

The humanistic view of motivation

Abraham Maslow earned his PhD in a psychology department that supported the behaviorist position. After he graduated, however, he came into contact with Gestalt psychologists (a group of German psychologists whose work during the 1920s and 1930s laid the foundation for the cognitive theories of the 1960s and 1970s), prepared for a career as a psychoanalyst, and became interested in anthropology. As a result of these various influences, he came to the conclusion that American psychologists who endorsed the behaviorist position had become so preoccupied with overt behavior and objectivity that they were ignoring other important aspects of human existence (hence the term *humanistic* to describe his views). When Maslow observed the behavior of especially well-adjusted persons – *self-actualizers,* as he called them – he concluded that healthy individuals are motivated to *seek* fulfilling experiences.

Maslow's theory of growth motivation

Maslow describes seventeen propositions, discussed in Chapter 1 of *Motivation and Personality* (3rd edn, 1987), that he believes would have to be incorporated into any sound theory of *growth motivation* (or *need gratification)* to meet them. Referring to need gratification as the most important single principle underlying all development, he adds that 'the single, holistic principle that binds together the multiplicity of human motives is the tendency for a new and higher need to emerge as the lower need fulfils itself by being sufficiently gratified' (1968: 55). He elaborates on this basic principle by proposing a five-level hierarchy of needs (see Figure 1 opposite).

Physiological needs are at the bottom of the hierarchy, followed in ascending order by *safety, belongingness and love, esteem,* and *self-actualization* needs. This order reflects differences in the relative strength of each need. The lower a need is in the hierarchy, the greater is its strength because when a lower-level need is activated (as in the case of extreme hunger or fear for one's physical safety) people will stop trying to satisfy a higher-level need (such as esteem or self-actualization) and focus on satisfying the currently active lower-level need (Maslow, 1987).

The first four needs (physiological, safety, belongingness & love, and esteem) are often referred to as 'deficiency' needs because they motivate people to act only when they are unmet to some degree. Self-actualization, by contrast, is often called a 'growth' need because people constantly strive to satisfy it. Basically, self-actualization refers to the need for self-fulfillment – the need to develop all of one's potential talents and capabilities. For example, an individual who felt she had the capability to write novels, teach, practice medicine, and raise children would not feel self-actualized until all of these goals had been accomplished to some minimal degree. Because it is at the top of the hierarchy and addresses the potential of the whole person, self-actualization is discussed more frequently than the other needs.

Maslow originally felt that self-actualization needs would automatically be activated as soon as esteem needs were met, but he changed his mind when he encountered individuals whose behavior did not fit this pattern. He concluded that individuals whose self-actualization needs became activated held in high regard such values as truth, goodness, beauty, justice, autonomy, and humor (Feist, 1990).

In addition to the five basic needs that compose the hierarchy, Maslow describes cognitive needs (such as the needs to know and to understand) and aesthetic needs

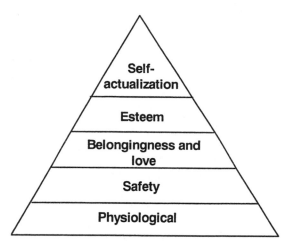

Figure 1 Maslow's hierarchy of human needs

(such as the needs for order, symmetry, or harmony). While not part of the basic hierarchy, these two classes of needs play a critical role in the satisfaction of basic needs. Maslow maintains that such conditions as the freedom to investigate and learn, fairness, honesty, and orderliness in interpersonal relationships are critical because their absence makes satisfaction of the five basic needs impossible. (Imagine, for example, trying to satisfy your belongingness and love needs or your esteem needs in an atmosphere characterized by dishonesty, unfair punishment, and restrictions on freedom of speech.)

Implications of Maslow's theory

The implications of Maslow's theory of motivation for teaching are provocative. One down-to-earth implication is that a teacher should do everything possible to see that the lower-level needs of students are satisfied so that they are more likely to function at the higher levels. Students are more likely to be primed to seek satisfaction of the esteem and self-actualization needs, for example, if they are physically comfortable, feel safe and relaxed, have a sense of belonging, and experience self-esteem. Only when the need for self-actualization is activated is a person likely to choose wisely when given the opportunity. Maslow emphasizes this point by making a distinction between *bad choosers* and *good choosers*. When some people are allowed freedom to choose, they seem consistently to make wise choices. Most people, however, frequently make self-destructive choices. An insecure student, for example, may choose to attend a particular college more on the basis of how close it is to home than on the quality of its academic programs.

Suggestions for teaching in your classroom

Motivating students to learn...

1. *Use behavioral techniques to help students exert themselves and work toward remote goals.*

Maslow's hierarchy of needs calls attention to the reasons that few students come to school bursting with eagerness to learn. Only students with all their deficiency needs satisfied are likely to experience a desire to know and understand. But even growth-motivated students may not fully appreciate the need to master certain basic skills before they can engage in more exciting and rewarding kinds of learning. And as we noted earlier, the information that appropriately administered reinforcement provides about one's level of competence contributes to high levels of self-esteem. Accordingly, you may often need to give your students incentives to learn...

2. *Make sure that students know what they are to do, how to proceed, and how to determine when they have achieved goals.*

Many times students do not exert themselves in the classroom because they say they don't know what they are supposed to do. Occasionally such a statement is merely an excuse for goofing off, but it may also be a legitimate explanation for lack of effort... Knowing what one is expected to do is important information in the construction of a learning strategy... In terms of motivation, objectives should be clear, understood by all members of the class, and attainable in a short period of time. For reasons illustrated by behavioral theorists' experiments with different reinforcement schedules, students are more likely to work steadily if they are reinforced at frequent intervals. If you set goals that are too demanding or remote, lack of reinforcement during the early stages of a unit may derail students, even if they started out with good intentions. Whenever you ask students to work toward a demanding or remote goal, try to set up a series of short-term goals.

3. *Do everything possible to satisfy deficiency needs – physiological, safety, belongingness, and esteem.*

a) Accommodate the instructional program to the physiological needs of your students.

b) Make your room physically and psychologically safe.

c) The need for safety is likely to be satisfied by the general classroom climate you establish, although physical factors of safety may be involved, particularly with young students...

d) Show your students that you take an interest in them and that they belong in your classroom.

e) Arrange learning experiences so that all students can gain at least a degree of esteem.

4. *Enhance the attractions and minimize the dangers of growth choices.*

When you first begin to teach, you might keep a copy of Maslow's diagram of a choice situation in your top desk drawer. Refer to it when the need arises, and ask yourself, 'Am I setting tasks up to encourage effort, or am I encouraging students *not* to try?' If you establish situations that generate pressure, tension, or anxiety, your students will choose safety and do their best to remain uninvolved. But if you minimize risks and make learning seem exciting and worthwhile, even the less secure students may join in.

Remain aware of the disadvantages of inappropriate or excessive competition. If competition becomes excessive in a school situation, students may think of learning only as a means to an end (being better than others or finishing first). As a result, students may become more interested in their relative position in a class than in their actual performance.

Only a few students will be able to experience success, and the tendency to make safety, rather than growth, choices will be increased. To avoid these disadvantages, encourage students to compete against themselves. Try to give each student some experience with success by arranging situations in which all students have a fairly equal chance in a variety of activities, and make use of group competitive situations that stress fun rather than winning.

5. *Direct learning experiences toward feelings of success in an effort to encourage an orientation toward achievement, a positive self-concept, and a strong sense of self-efficacy.*

To feel successful, an individual must first establish goals that are neither so low as to be unfulfilling nor so high as to be impossible, and then know that the goals have been achieved. This is a two-step process: establishing goals and receiving knowledge of results.

a) Make use of objectives that are challenging but attainable and, when appropriate, that involve student input.

Although in many instructional situations, you may find it necessary to set goals yourself, when it is possible and instructionally appropriate, you can use goals to heighten motivation as well. In these instances you are likely to get a better reaction if you invite your students to participate in selecting objectives or at least in thinking along with you as you explain why the objectives are worthwhile. This will tend to shift the emphasis from extrinsic to intrinsic motivation.

To help students suggest appropriate objectives, you may want to use the techniques recommended by Robert Mager. You might assist your students in stating objectives in terms of a time limit, a minimum number of correct responses, a proportion of correct responses, or a sample of actions.

b) Provide knowledge of results by emphasizing the positive.

To experience success (as a basis for establishing a realistic level of aspiration), your students must receive detailed information about their performance. Comments on the quality of a presentation, participation in a debate, papers and projects of various kinds, or answers on an exam may make the difference between feelings of success and feelings of failure. Accordingly, you should do your best to comment favorably on successful performance and avoid calling attention to failure, particularly the kind that is already apparent.

Behavioral theorists have proposed that for praise to shape behavior, it should be provided only after performance of designated activities, and it should be specific. Humanistic theorists (Purkey & Stanley, 1991; 1994) add that it should be sincere and credible. Jere Brophy (1981), however, suggests that classroom teachers rarely use praise as an effective or desirable form of reinforcement. Brophy recommends that teachers use praise in the following ways:

131

- As a spontaneous expression of surprise or admiration. ('Why, Juan! This report is really excellent!')

- As compensation for criticism or as vindication of a prediction. ('After your last report, Lily, I said I knew you could do better. Well, you *have* done better. This is really excellent.')

- As an attempt to impress all members of a class. ('I like the way Nguyen just put his books away so promptly.')

- As a transition ritual to verify that an assignment has been completed. ('Yes, Maya, that's very good. You can work on your project now.')

- As a consolation prize or as encouragement to students who are less capable than others. ('Well, Josh, you kept at it, and you got it finished. Good for you!')

Many of these uses of praise do not serve to reinforce student behavior in specific ways. Quite often, however, various forms of praise may influence a student's self-concept and attitude toward learning. High achievers tend to attribute failure to lack of effort and resolve to try harder. Low achievers often attribute failure to lack of ability and assume nothing can be done about it. Brophy suggests that teachers may shape such reactions by the ways they supply praise (and criticism).

6. *Try to encourage the development of need achievement, self-confidence, and self-direction in students who need these qualities.*

Despite your efforts to provide appropriate incentives, gratify deficiency needs, enhance the attractions of growth choices, and arrange learning experiences to produce a realistic level of aspiration and a feeling of success, some of your students will still lack confidence in their ability to learn. In such cases you may try to help students acquire a general motive to achieve.

a) Use achievement-motivation training techniques.

A technique described by John Nicholls (1979) allows students opportunities to schedule their own classroom learning. For example, students can be given responsibility for deciding when to work on a particular assignment and for how long. This gives them the feeling they are working on a task because they want to, not because someone told them to. According to Nicholls, researchers have found greater continuing interest in learning tasks under self-evaluation and greater frequencies of assignment completion when opportunities for self-scheduling were increased.

b) Use co-operative-learning methods.

… Co-operative-learning methods have proven effective in increasing motivation for learning and self-esteem, redirecting attributions for success and failure, fostering positive feelings toward classmates, and increasing performance on tests of comprehension, reasoning, and problem solving (Johnson & Johnson, 1995; Johnson *et al.* 1995; Slavin, 1995). Accordingly, you may want to try one or more of the co-operative-learning techniques described by Johnson and Johnson (Johnson *et al.* 1994) and Slavin (1995). To familiarize you with these methods, we will briefly describe the Student Teams Achievement Divisions (STAD) method devised by Slavin and his associates at Johns Hopkins University.

STAD is one of the simplest and most flexible of the co-operative-learning methods, having been used in grades 2 through 12 and in such diverse subject areas as math, language arts, social studies, and science. As with other co-operative-learning methods, students are assigned to four- or five-member groups, with each group mirroring the make-up of the class in terms of ability, background, and gender. Once these assignments are made, a four-step cycle is initiated: teach, team study, test, and recognition. The teaching phase begins with the presentation of material, usually in a lecture-discussion format. Students should be told what it is they are going to learn and why it is important. During team study, group members work co-operatively with teacher-provided worksheets and answer sheets. Next, each student *individually* takes a quiz. Using a scoring system that ranges from 0 to 30 points and reflects degree of individual improvement over previous quiz scores, the teacher scores the papers. Each team receives one of three recognition awards, depending on the average number of points earned by the team. For example, teams that average 15 to 19 improvement points receive a GOODTEAM certificate, teams that average 20 to 24 improvement points receive a GREATTEAM certificate, and teams that average 25 to 30 improvement points receive a SUPERTEAM certificate.

The co-operative methods developed by the Johnsons are similar to those developed by Slavin, but with two exceptions: these methods place a greater emphasis on teaching students how to work productively together, and they recommend using team grades, rather than certificates or other forms of recognition, as positive reinforcers.

7. *Try to make learning interesting by emphasizing activity, investigation, adventure, social interaction, and usefulness.*

More than twenty-five years ago, May Seagoe suggested an approach to motivation that is based on students' interests and that is consistent with many of the motivation theories mentioned in this chapter. Among the 'points of appeal that emerge from studies of specific interests,' she lists the following:

a) *the opportunity for overt bodily activity, for manipulation, for construction, even for observing the movement of animals and vehicles of various sorts;*

b) *the opportunity for investigation, for using mental ingenuity in solving puzzles, for working problems through, for creating designs, and the like;*

c) *the opportunity for adventure, for vicarious experiences in make believe, in books, and in the mass media;*

d) *the opportunity for social assimilation, for contacts with others suitable to the maturity level of the child (ranging from parallel play to discussion and argument), for social events and working together, for human interest and humanitarianism, and for conformity and display; and*

e) *the opportunity for use of the new in real life, making the new continuous with past experience and projecting it in terms of future action.* (1970: 25)

One approach that incorporates most or all of these features ... is the project approach. Lillian Katz and Sylvia Chard (1989) define a project as an in-depth study of a particular topic that one or more children undertake and that extends over a period of days or weeks. Projects may involve an initial discussion that captures the students' interest (for example, discussing how a house is built); dramatic play; drawing, painting, and writing; group discussions; field trips; construction activities; and investigation activities. Because projects are based on children's natural interests and involve a wide range of activities, they are more likely to be intrinsically motivating.

As you think about how you are going to organize your lesson plans for each day and each period, you might ask yourself: 'Are there ways that I can incorporate activity, investigation, adventure, social interaction, and usefulness into this presentation?' 'Are there projects that I can assign to students, particularly as co-operative groups, that incorporate most of these features?'

References

Anderman EM & Maehr ML (1994) 'Motivations and schooling in the middle grades' *Review of Educational Research* 64 (2), pp287–309

Atkinson J (1964) *An introduction to motivation* Van Nostrand

Brophy JE (1981) 'Teacher praise: a functional analysis' *Review of Educational Research* 51 (1), pp5–32

Cain KM & Dweck CS (1995) 'The relation between motivational patterns and achievement cognitions through the elementary school years' *Merrill-Palmer Quarterly* 41 (1), pp25–52

Cameron J & Pierce WD (1994) 'Reinforcement, reward and intrinsic motivation: a meta-analysis' *Review of Educational Research* 64 (3), pp363–423

Chance P (1992) 'The rewards of learning' *Phi Delta Kappan* 74 (3), pp200–207

Covington MV (1985) 'Strategic thinking and the fear of failure' in JW Segal, SF Chipman & R Glaser (eds) *Thinking and learning skills* (vol 1) Lawrence Erlbaum

deCharms R (1976) *Enhancing motivation: change in the classroom* Irvington

Feist J (1990) *Theories of personality* 2nd edn Holt, Rinehart & Winston

Glasser W (1986) *Control theory in the classroom* Harper & Row

Glasser W (1990) *The quality school* Harper & Row

Graham S & Weiner B (1993) 'Attributional applications in the classroom' in TM Tomlinson (ed) *Motivating students to learn: overcoming barriers to high achievement* McCutchan

Henderson VL & Dweck CS (1990) 'Motivation and achievement' in SS Feldman & GR Elliott (eds) *At the threshold: the developing adolescent* Harvard University Press

Johnson DW & Johnson RT (1995) 'Cooperative learning and non academic outcomes of schooling: the other side of the report card' in JE Pederson & AD Digby (eds) *Secondary schools and cooperative learning* Garland

Johnson DW, Johnson RT & Holubec EJ (1994) *The new circles of learning: cooperation in the classroom and school* Association for Supervision and Curriculum Development

Johnson DW, Johnson RT & Smith KA (1995) 'Cooperative learning and individual student achievement in secondary schools' in JE Pederson & AD Digby (eds) *Secondary schools and cooperative learning* Garland

Katz L & Chard S (1989) *Engaging children's minds: the project approach* Ablex Publishing

Kohn A (1993) 'Rewards versus learning: a response to Paul Chance' *Phi Delta Kappan* 76 (4), pp272–283

Maslow AH (1968) *Towards a psychology of being* 2nd edn Van Nostrand

Maslow AH (1987) *Motivation and personality* 3rd edn Harper & Row

Morgan M (1984) 'Reward-induced decrements and increments in intrinsic motivation' *Review of Educational Research* 54 (1), pp5–30

Nicholls JG (1979) 'Quality and inequality in intellectual development: the role of motivation in education' *American Psychologist* 34 (11), pp1071–1084

Purkey WW & Stanley PH (1991) *Invitational teaching, learning and living* National Educational Association

Purkey WW & Stanley PH (1994) *The inviting school treasury: 1001 ways to invite student success* Scholastic

Seagoe MV (1970) *The learning process and school practice* Chandler

Slavin RE (1995) *Cooperative learning: theory, research and practice* 2nd edn Allyn & Bacon

Stipek DJ (1993) *Motivation to learn: from theory to practice* 2nd edn Allyn & Bacon

8.   Classroom Management

Robert Biehler & Jack Snowman

By now you have no doubt begun to realize that teaching is a complex enterprise. It is complex for the following reasons:

- Students vary in their physical, social, emotional, cognitive, and cultural characteristics.

- Systematic preparations have to be made to ensure that students master the objectives that teachers lay out.

- Learning occurs gradually and openly with extensive and varied practice.

- Different students learn at different rates.

- Students are motivated to learn (or not learn) by different factors.

- Learning can be measured and evaluated in a variety of ways.

If not managed properly, an endeavor as complex as teaching can easily become chaotic... [You] will have to become familiar with different ways of managing the various behaviors that your students will exhibit. To appreciate the role you will play as the manager of a diverse group of students, think of yourself as the equivalent of an orchestra. An orchestra is, of course, a collection of musicians who vary in terms of the instrument they play, the years of experience they have, the way they prefer to play, and how they think a particular piece should sound. It is the conductor's job to understand all these factors and manage them in such a way that the outcome is a performance that pleases both performer and audience.

Before describing the various management techniques that you may have reason to use at one time or another, we would like to make you aware of several general factors that influence how students behave in classrooms: the types of tasks you assign, the structure you provide for these tasks, and the learning goals you choose to emphasize.

First, you should realize that the types of learning tasks your students are assigned can affect their behavior in class. Behavior problems are often related to learning tasks that are characterized by a high degree of ambiguity ... and that carry with them a high risk, such as of receiving a poor grade. But don't avoid engaging your students in such tasks because many of the learning tasks you most want your students to undertake inevitably involve these two characteristics. For instance, most application and problem-solving tasks are high in both ambiguity and risk (Doyle, 1983). Instead, present such tasks to your students in a way that lessens their discomfort. Students who understand what is expected of them, see the task as a meaningful one, and feel as confident as possible that they have the skills to meet challenging demands are less likely to be behavior problems...

Second, recognize that a traditional view of a well-managed classroom, which includes the notions of students working silently at their desks (or in front of their computers), speaking only when spoken to, and providing verbatim recitations of what the teacher and textbook said, is incompatible with ... contemporary views of learning and motivation... If some of your goals are for students to acquire a meaningful knowledge base, to become proficient problem solvers, and to learn how to work productively with others, then you have to accept the idea that these goals are best met in classrooms that are characterized by a fair amount of autonomy, physical movement, and social interaction (McCaslin & Good, 1992).

Authoritarian, laissez-faire, and authoritative approaches to classroom management

... Diana Baumrind (1971; 1991) found that parents tended to exhibit one of three styles in managing the behavior of their children: authoritarian, laissez-faire (or permissive), or authoritative. These three styles can be applied as well to a teacher's actions in the classroom. We will quickly review Baumrind's categories and then take a brief look at how teachers' approaches to management, too, can be characterized by these styles.

Authoritarian parents establish rules for their children's behavior and expect them to be blindly obeyed. Explanations of why a particular rule is necessary are almost never given. Instead, rewards and punishments are given for following or not following rules. *Laissez-faire* parents represent the other extreme. They impose few controls. They allow their children to make many basic decisions (such as what to eat, what to dress, when to go to bed) and provide advice or assistance only when asked. *Authoritative* parents provide rules but discuss the reasons for them, teach their children how to meet them, and reward children for exhibiting self-control. Authoritative parents also cede more responsibility for self-governance to their children as the children demonstrate increased self-regulation skills. This style, more so than the other two, leads to internalization of the parents' norms and to maintenance of intrinsic motivation for following them in the future.

You can probably see the parallel between Baumrind's work and classroom management. Teachers who adopt an authoritarian style tend to have student compliance as their main goal ('Do what I say because I say so') and make heavy use of rewards and punishments to produce that compliance. Teachers who adopt a permissive style rely heavily on students identifying with and respecting them as their main approach to classroom management ('Do what I say because you like me and respect my judgement'). Teachers who adopt an authoritative style have as their main goal students who can eventually regulate their own behavior. By explaining the rationale for classroom rules and by adjusting those rules as students demonstrate the ability to appropriately govern themselves, authoritative teachers hope to convince students that adopting the teacher's norms for classroom behavior as their own will lead to the achievement of valued academic goals ('Do what I say because doing so will help you learn more'). The students of authoritative teachers better understand the need for classroom rules and tend to operate within them most of the time (McCaslin & Good, 1992).

138

The first part of this chapter will describe guidelines you might follow to establish and maintain an effective learning environment... Even if you do an excellent job of 'getting it all together,' however, certain factors and conditions will be beyond your control. Inevitably, some students will fail to respond to your efforts as positively as others. Accordingly, you will occasionally need to deal with disruptive behavior. The second part of this chapter will describe a variety of techniques you might use to handle such types of behavior and will conclude with an analysis on the reasons for school violence. The emphasis in both parts will be on helping you become an authoritative manager of classroom behavior.

Preventing problems: techniques of classroom management

Kounin's observations on group management

Interest in the significance of classroom management was kindled when Jacob Kounin wrote a book titled *Discipline and Group Management in Classrooms* (1970). Kounin noted that he first became interested in group management when he reprimanded a college student for blatantly reading a newspaper in class. Kounin was struck by the extent to which the entire class responded to a reprimand directed at only one person, and he subsequently dubbed this the 'ripple effect'. Chances are you can recall a situation when you were diligently working away in a classroom and the teacher suddenly became quite angry at a disruptive classmate. If you felt a bit tense after the incident (even though your behavior was blameless) and tried to give the impression that you were a paragon of student virtue, you have had personal experience with the ripple effect.

Once his interest in classroom behavior was aroused, Kounin supervised a series of observational and experimental studies of student reactions to techniques of teacher control. In analyzing the results of these various studies, he came to the conclusion that the following classroom management techniques appear to be most effective.

1. *Show your students that you are 'with it'.* Kounin coined the term withitness to emphasize that teachers who prove to their students that they know what is going on in a classroom usually have fewer behavior problems than teachers who appear to be unaware of incipient disruptions. An expert at classroom management will nip trouble in the bud by commenting on potentially disruptive behavior before it gains momentum. An ineffective teacher may not notice such behavior until it begins to spread and then perhaps hopes that it will simply go away. At first glance Kounin's suggestion that you show that you are with it might seem to be in conflict with operant conditioning's prediction that non-reinforced behavior will disappear. If the teacher's reaction is the only source of reinforcement in a classroom, ignoring behavior may cause it to disappear. In many cases, however, a misbehaving student gets reinforced by the reactions of classmates. Therefore, ignoring behavior is much less likely to lead to extinction of a response in a classroom than in controlled experimental situations.

2. *Learn to cope with overlapping situations.* When he analyzed video-tapes of actual classroom interactions, Kounin found that some teachers seemed to have one-track minds. They were inclined to deal with only one thing at a time, and this

way of proceeding caused frequent interruptions in classroom routine. One primary grade teacher observed by Kounin, for example, was working with a reading group when she noticed two boys on the other side of the room poking each other. She abruptly got up, walked over to the boys, berated them at length, and then returned to the reading group. By the time she returned, however, the children in the reading group had become bored and listless and were tempted to engage in mischief of their own.

Kounin concluded that withitness and skill in handling overlapping activities seemed to be related. An expert classroom manager who is talking to children in a reading group, for example, might notice two boys at the far side of the room who are beginning to scuffle with each other. Such a teacher might in mid-sentence tell the boys to stop and make the point so adroitly that the attention of the children in the reading group does not waver. You might carry out a self-analysis of how you handle overlapping situations when you first begin to teach. If you find that you tend to focus on only one thing at a time, you might make an effort to develop skills in coping with two or more situations simultaneously.

3. *Strive to maintain smoothness and momentum in class activities.* This point is related to the previous one. Kounin found that some teachers caused problems for themselves by constantly interrupting activities without thinking about what they were doing. Some teachers whose activities were recorded on videotape failed to maintain the thrust of a lesson because they seemed unaware of the rhythm of student behavior (that is, they did not take into account the degree of student inattention and restlessness but instead moved ahead in an almost mechanical way). Others flip-flopped from one activity to another. Still others would interrupt one activity (for example, a reading lesson) to comment on an unrelated aspect of classroom functioning ('Someone left a lunch bag on the floor'). There were also some who wasted time dwelling on a trivial incident (making a big fuss because a boy lost his pencil). And a few teachers delivered individual, instead of group, instructions ('All right, Charlie, you go to the board. Fine. Now, Rebecca, you go to the board'). All these types of teacher behavior tended to interfere with the flow of learning activities. You might carry out a movement analysis of your own teaching from time to time. Think about how you handle a class for a period or a day, and see if you can recall incidents of the sort just described. To counteract such tendencies, you might endeavor to maintain a smooth flow of activities in the following class periods and days. If you succeed in doing so, this smooth flow may become habitual.

4. *Try to keep the whole class involved, even when you are dealing with individual students.* Kounin found that some well-meaning teachers had fallen into a pattern of calling on students in a predictable order and in such a way that the rest of the class served as a passive audience. Unless you stop to think about what you are doing during group recitation periods, you might easily fall into the same trap. If you do, the 'audience' is almost certain to become bored and may be tempted to engage in troublemaking activities just to keep occupied. Some teachers, for example, call on students to recite by going around a circle, or going up and down

rows, or by following alphabetical order. Others call on a child first and then ask a question. Still others ask one child to recite at length (read an entire page, for example). All these techniques tend to spotlight one child in predictable order and cause the rest of the class members to tune out until their turn comes. You are more likely to maintain interest and limit mischief caused by boredom if you use techniques such as the following:

- Ask a question, and after pausing a few seconds to let everyone think about it, pick out someone to answer it. With subsequent questions, call on students in an unpredictable order so that no one knows when she will be asked to recite. (If you feel that some students in a class are very apprehensive about being called on, even under relaxing circumstances, you can either ask them extremely easy questions or avoid calling on them at all.)

- If you single out one child to go to the board to do a problem, ask all other students to do the same problem at their desks, and then choose one or two at random to compare their work with the answers on the board.

- When dealing with lengthy or complex material, call on several students in quick succession (and in unpredictable order), and ask each to handle one section. In a primary grade reading group, for example, have one child read a sentence; then pick someone at the other side of the group to read the next sentence and so on.

- Use props in the form of flashcards, mimeographed sheets, or work-book pages to induce all students to respond to questions simultaneously. Then, ask students to compare answers. (One ingenious elementary school teacher observed by Kounin had each student print the ten digits on cards that could be inserted in a slotted piece of cardboard. She would ask a question such as 'How much is 8 and 4?'; she would pause a moment while the students arranged their answers in the slots and then say, 'All show!')

5. *Introduce variety, and be enthusiastic, particularly with younger students.* After viewing videotapes of different teachers, Kounin and his associates concluded that some teachers seemed to fall into a deadly routine much more readily than others. They followed the same procedure day after day and responded with the same, almost reflexive comments. At the other end of the scale were teachers who introduced variety, responded with enthusiasm and interest, and moved quickly to new activities when they sensed that students either had mastered or were satiated by a particular lesson. It seems logical to assume that students will be less inclined to sleep, daydream, or engage in disruptive activities if they are exposed to an enthusiastic teacher who varies the pace and type of classroom activities. Kounin pointed out, however, that variety may be most appropriate in elementary school classrooms because older students may be interested in thoroughly analyzing complex ideas and may be bothered if they are interrupted too frequently.

6. *Be aware of the ripple effect. When criticizing student behavior, be clear and firm, focus on behavior rather than on personalities, and try to avoid angry outbursts.* If you take into account the suggestions just made, you may be able to reduce the

141

amount of student misbehavior in your classes. Even so, some behavior problems are certain to occur. When you deal with these, you can benefit from Kounin's research on the ripple effect. On the basis of observations, questionnaires, and experimental evidence, he concluded that 'innocent' students in a class are more likely to be positively impressed by the way the teacher handles a misbehavior if the following conditions exist:

- The teacher identifies the misbehaver and states what the unacceptable behavior is. ('Jorge! Don't flip that computer disk at Jamal.')

- The teacher specifies a more constructive behavior. ('Please put the computer disk back in the storage box.')

- The teacher explains why the deviant behavior should cease. ('If the computer disk gets broken or dirty, no one else will be able to use it, and we'll have to get a new one.')

- The teacher is firm and authoritative and conveys a no-nonsense attitude. ('[Breaking] classroom rules will result in an appropriate punishment – no ifs, ands, or buts.')

- The teacher does not resort to anger, humiliation, or extreme punishment. Kounin concludes that extreme reactions did not seem to make children behave better. Instead, anger and severe reprimands upset them and made them feel tense and nervous. ('Roger, I am deeply disappointed that you used obscene language in your argument with Michael. Such behavior is simply unacceptable in my classroom.')

- The teacher focuses on behavior, not on personality. (Say, 'Ramona, staring out the window instead of reading your textbook is unacceptable behavior in my classroom' rather than 'Ramona, you're the laziest student I have ever had in class.')

University of Texas studies of group management

Stimulated by Kounin's observations, members of the Research and Development Center for Teacher Education at the University of Texas at Austin instituted a series of studies on classroom management. The basic procedure followed in most studies was to first identify very effective and less effective teachers by using a variety of criteria (often stressing student achievement), ratings, and observations. Then classroom management techniques used by very effective teachers were analyzed in detail. In some studies (for example, Brophy, 1979; Good, 1982) basic characteristics of well-managed classrooms were described. They can be summarized as follows:

1. Students know what they are expected to do and generally experience the feeling that they are successful doing it.

2. Students are kept busy engaging in teacher-led instructional activities.

3. There is little wasted time, confusion, or disruption.

4. A no-nonsense, work-orientated tone prevails, but at the same time there is a relaxed and pleasant atmosphere.

The first point can be interpreted as supporting the use of instructional objectives that are stated in such a way that students know when they have achieved them. It might also be interpreted as supporting the use of mastery learning evaluation procedure. The next three points stress student productivity under teacher guidance and a non-nonsense, work-orientated atmosphere. These outcomes are more likely when teachers use procedures recommended by behavioral and cognitive psychologists.

Another set of studies carried out by the Texas researchers led to two recent books on group management, one for elementary school teachers (Evertson, Emmer, Clements & Worsham, 1994) and the other for secondary school teachers (Emmer, Evertson, Clements & Worsham, 1994)... We will provide the following summary of basic keys to management success stressed in both volumes:

1. On the first day with a new class, very effective teachers clearly demonstrate that they have thought about classroom procedures ahead of time. They have planned first-day activities that make it possible for classroom routine to be handled with a minimum of confusion. They also make sure students understand why the procedures are necessary and how they are to be followed.

2. A short list of basic classroom rules is posted/and or announced, and students are told about the penalties they will incur in the event of misbehavior.

3. During the first weeks with a new group of students, effective teachers have students engage in whole-group activities under teacher direction. Such activities are selected to make students feel comfortable and successful in their new classroom.

4. After the initial shakedown period is over, effective teachers maintain control by using the sorts of techniques described by Kounin; that show they are with it, cope with overlapping situations, maintain smoothness and momentum, and avoid ignoring the rest of the class when dealing with individual students.

5. Effective teachers give clear directions, hold students accountable for completing assignments, and give frequent feedback.

Assertive discipline

This list of factors calls attention to the importance of being thoroughly prepared the first days you meet with a new class. You should not only have thought about how you are going to handle classroom routine; you should also have planned learning activities likely to make students feel comfortable and successful. You should give students clear assignments, convey the message that they will be responsible for completing them, and provide supportive feedback so that they are aware they have completed work successfully. A specific version of this general approach is the Assertive Discipline program of Lee Canter (1989).

Canter's program has three parts and is modeled after the classroom management practices of master teachers. The first part, *teaching students how to behave,* has two general steps. First, establish specific directions for each activity. For an all-class discussion, for example, you may want students to raise their hands and be recognized before speaking. For a co-operative-learning session, you may want students to stay in their seats and work quietly. Second, make sure students know how to behave. You can accomplish this by writing the desired behaviors on the board, demonstrating them, asking students to restate them, questioning students to verify that they understand the rules, and immediately engaging them in the activity.

The second part of Assertive Discipline is *providing positive reinforcement* for good behavior. Canter suggests that whenever you notice a student who is following the rules, point it out and compliment her. For example, if Maria has followed the rules laid down for a class discussion, you might say, 'Maria raised her hand and patiently waited to be called on. Very good, Maria.' Although this part of the program is either omitted or de-emphasized by some teachers, Canter feels it is as important as the other two parts.

The third and final part of the program is *invoking the discipline plan*. This involves the use of aversive consequences, but only after students have been taught the desired behaviors and positive reinforcement has been given. Canter suggests that teachers refrain from using aversive consequences until at least two students have been positively reinforced for behaving appropriately. A discipline plan should include no more than five aversive consequences for misbehavior, each of which is slightly more severe than the last one. For example, the first time a rule is broken, the student is warned. The second and third infractions result in ten-minute and fifteen-minute time-outs, respectively. The fourth infraction results in a call to the parents. And if the rule is broken a fifth time, the student must visit the principal. Although there are a variety of aversive consequences that you can use, avoid those that might cause psychological or physical harm (ridicule, for example)...

Managing the middle, junior high, and high school classroom

Most of the classroom management techniques and suggestions we have discussed so far are sufficiently general that they can be used in a variety of classroom settings and with primary through secondary grade students. Nevertheless, teaching pre-adolescents and adolescents is sufficiently different from teaching younger students that the management of the middle school, junior high, and high school classroom requires a slightly different emphasis and a few unique practices.

Classroom management has to be approached somewhat differently in the secondary grades (and in those middle schools that change classes several times a day) because of the segmented nature of education for these grades. Instead of being in charge of the same twenty-five to thirty students all day, most junior high or high school teachers (and some middle school teachers) are responsible for as many as five different groups of twenty-five to thirty students for about fifty minutes each. This arrangement results in a wider range of individual differences, a greater likelihood that these teachers will see a wide range of behavior problems, and a greater concern with efficient use of class time.

Because of the special nature of adolescence, relatively short class times, and consecutive classes with different students, middle school, junior high, and high school teachers must concentrate their efforts on preventing misbehavior. Edmund Emmer, Carolyn Evertson, Barbara Clements, and Murray Worsham (1994), in *Classroom Management for Secondary Teachers* (3rd edn), discuss how teachers can prevent misbehavior by carefully organizing the classroom environment, establishing clear rules and procedures, and delivering effective instruction.

According to Emmer and his associates, the physical features of the classroom should be arranged to optimize teaching and learning. They suggest an environment in which (1) the arrangement of the seating, materials, and equipment is consistent with the kinds of instructional activities the teacher favors; (2) high traffic areas, such as the teacher's desk and the pencil sharpener, are kept free of congestion; (3) the teacher can easily see all students; (4) frequently used teaching materials and student supplies are readily available; and (5) students can easily see instructional presentations and displays.

In too many instances teachers spend a significant amount of class time dealing with misbehavior, rather than with teaching and learning, either because students are never told what is expected of them or because rules and procedures are not communicated clearly. Accordingly, Emmer *et al.* suggest that classroom rules be specifically stated, discussed with students on the first day of class, and, for seventh, eighth, and ninth grades, posted in a prominent place. Sophomores, juniors, and seniors should be given a handout on which the rules are listed. Some examples of these basic rules follow:

- Bring all needed materials to class.
- Be in your seat and ready to work when the bell rings.
- Respect and be polite to all people.
- Do not talk or leave your desk when someone else is talking.
- Respect other people's property.
- Obey all school rules.

You may also want to allow some degree of student participation in rule setting. You can ask students to suggest rules, arrange for students to discuss why certain classroom rules are necessary, and perhaps allow students to select a few rules. This last suggestion should be taken up cautiously, however. Because middle school and secondary teachers teach different sets of students, having a different set of rules for each class is bound to cause confusion for you and hard feelings among some students. You may find yourself admonishing a student for breaking a rule that applies to a different class, and some students will naturally want to know why they cannot do something that is allowed in another class.

In addition to rules, various procedures need to be formulated and communicated. Procedures differ from rules in that they apply to a specific activity and are usually directed at completing a task rather than completing a behavior. To produce a well-run classroom, you will need to formulate efficient procedures for beginning-of-the-period tasks (such as taking attendance and allowing students to leave the classroom), use of materials and equipment (such as the encyclopaedia, dictionary, and pencil sharpener), learning activities (such as discussions, seatwork, and group work), and end-of-the-period tasks (such as handing in seatwork assignments, returning materials and equipment, and making announcements).

Much of what Emmer and his associates mention in relation to the characteristics of effective instruction has been described in earlier chapters. For example, they recommend that short-term (daily, weekly) and long-term (semester, annual) lesson plans be formulated and co-ordinated, that instructions and standards for assignments be clear and given in a timely manner, that feedback be given at regular intervals, and that the grading system be clear and fairly applied.

The following Suggestions for Teaching will help you become an effective manager of student behavior in the classroom.

Suggestions for teaching in your classroom

Techniques of classroom management

1. *Show you are confident and prepared the first day of class.*

The first few minutes with any class are often crucial. Your students will be sizing you up, especially if they know you are a new teacher. If you act scared and unsure of yourself, you will probably be in for trouble. Even after years of experience, you may find that confronting a roomful of strange students for the first time is a bit intimidating. You will be the center of attention and may feel the equivalent of stage fright. To switch the focus of attention and to begin identifying your students as individuals rather than as a threatening audience, you might consider using this strategy. Hand out 4-by-6-inch cards as soon as everyone is seated, and ask your students to write down their full names, the names they prefer to be called, what their hobbies and favorite activities are, and a description of the most interesting experience they have ever had.

As they write, you will be in a position to make a leisurely scrutiny of your students as individuals. Recognizing that you are dealing with individuals should reduce the tendency to feel threatened by a group. Perhaps you have read about singers who pick out a single, sympathetic member of the audience and sing directly to her. The sea of faces as a whole is frightening. The face of the individual is not. Even if you are not bothered by being the center of attention, you might still consider using this card technique to obtain information that you can use to learn names rapidly and to individualize instruction. Whatever you do during the first few minutes, it is important to give the impression that you know exactly what you are doing. The best way to pull that off is to be thoroughly prepared.

2. *Think ahead about how you plan to handle classroom routine, and explain basic procedures the first few minutes of the first day.*

The Texas researchers found that very effective teachers demonstrated from the first moment with a new group of students that they knew how to handle the details of their job. They also conveyed the impression that they expected co-operation. To demonstrate that you are a confident, competent instructor, you should plan exactly how you will handle classroom routines. You will pick up at least some ideas about the details of classroom management during student-teaching experiences, but it might be worth asking a friendly experienced teacher in your school for advice about tried-and-true procedures that have worked in that particular school.

Try to anticipate how you will handle such details as taking attendance, assigning desks, handing out books and materials, permitting students to go to the restroom during class, and so forth. If you don't plan ahead, you will have to come up with an improvised policy on the spur of the moment, and that policy might turn out to be highly inefficient or in conflict with school regulations.

3. *Establish class rules, call attention to them, and explain why they are necessary.*

Very effective teachers observed by the Texas researchers demonstrated an authoritative approach to classroom management by explaining class rules the first day of school. Some teachers list standard procedures on a chart or bulletin board; others simply state them the first day of class. Either technique saves time and trouble later because all you have to do is refer to the rule when a transgression occurs. The alternative to this approach is to interrupt the lesson and disturb the whole class while you make a hurried, unplanned effort to deal with a surprise attack. Your spur-of-the-moment reaction may turn out to be clumsy and ineffective.

When you introduce rules the first day, take a positive, non-threatening approach. If you spit rules out as if they were a series of ultimatums, students may feel you have a chip on your shoulder, which the unwritten code of the classroom obligates them to try knocking off. One way to demonstrate your good faith is to invite the class to suggest necessary regulations and explain why they should be established. Whatever your approach, encourage understanding of the reasons for the rules. You can make regulations seem desirable, rather than restrictive, if you discuss why they are needed. Reasonable rules are much more likely to be remembered and honored than pronouncements that seem to be the whims of a tyrant.

4. *Begin class work the first day with an instructional activity that is clearly stated and can be completed quickly and successfully.*

When selecting the very first assignment to give to a new class, refer to the suggestions for preparing instructional objectives proposed by Robert Mager and Norman Gronlund, and arrange a short assignment that can be successfully completed before the end of the period. Clearly specify what is to be done, and perhaps state the conditions and criteria for determining successful completion. In addition, mention an activity (such as examining the assigned text) that students should engage in after they have completed the assignment. In the elementary grades, you might give a short assignment that helps students review material covered in the preceding grade. At the secondary level, pick out an initial assignment that is short, interesting, and does not depend on technical knowledge.

5. *During the first weeks with a new group of students, have them spend most of their time engaging in whole-class activities under your direction.*

The very effective teachers observed by the Texas researchers followed the strategy just described, which makes sense when you stop to think about it. You can't expect students to adjust to the routine of a new teacher and classroom in just a few days. Accordingly, it would be wise to make sure students have settled down before asking them to engage in relatively unstructured activities like discovery learning.

Furthermore, group discussions or cooperative-learning arrangements usually work out more successfully when the participants have a degree of familiarity with one another and a particular set of background factors (such as a chapter in a text). Thus, as you plan activities during the first weeks with a new class, prepare instructional objectives that ask students to complete assignments under your direction. Postpone using the techniques just mentioned until later in the report period.

6. Give clear instructions, hold students accountable for carrying them out, and provide frequent feedback.

All three of these goals can be achieved by making systematic use of instructional objectives ... and by putting into practice the model of instruction described throughout this book.

7. Continually demonstrate that you are competent, well prepared, and in charge.

As students work at achieving instructional objectives, participate in group discussions, or engage in any other kind of learning activity, show them that you are a competent classroom manager. Arrange periods so that there will be a well-organized transition from one activity to the next, maintain smoothness and momentum, and don't waste time. Use a variety of teaching approaches so that you please some of your students some of the time, and use techniques recommended by behavioral, cognitive, and humanistic psychologists. Show you are with it by being alert for signs of mischief or disruptive behavior.

8. Be professional but pleasant, and try to establish a businesslike but supportive classroom atmosphere.

If you establish classroom routines in a competent fashion and keep your students busy working to achieve clearly stated instructional objectives, you should be able to establish a no-nonsense, productive atmosphere. At the same time, you should strive to make your room an inviting and pleasant place to be. Keep in mind the points made regarding the importance of self-esteem, self-efficacy, and interpersonal relationships. Put yourself in the place of students thrust into a strange classroom with an unfamiliar instructor. Try to identify with your students so that you can appreciate how they feel if they do or say something embarrassing or have difficulty with class work.

One of the best ways to get students to respond positively to you and make them feel welcome in your classroom is to learn their names as quickly as possible (even if you have five sections of secondary school students to teach). To accomplish this feat, refer to the cards mentioned in point 1. Use the information that students have provided, perhaps supplemented by your own notes or sketches about distinctive physical and facial features, to establish associations between names and faces. Before and after every class period the first few days, flip through your pile of cards, try to picture the appearance of the students, and practice using their names... Once you have learned a student's name, use it as often as possible to maintain the memory trace. Greet students by name as they come in the door, use their names when asking them to recite or carry out some task, and speak to them personally when you hand back assignments.

Another way to make students feel at home in your classroom is to try establishing a feeling of class spirit. One way to do this is to have a brief *sharing* period – similar to the sharing time you may remember from your kindergarten days at the beginning of each period. Invite students to describe recent interesting experiences they have had or to give announcements about extracurricular activities. If a member of the class is injured in an accident or suffers a lengthy illness, buy a get-well card, and have every member of the class sign it before sending it off.

References

Baumrind D (1971) 'Current patterns of parental authority' *Developmental Psychology Monographs* 4 (1, Pt 2), 1–103

Baumrind D (1991) 'Parenting styles and adolescent development' in RM Learner, AC Peterson & J Brooks-Gunn (eds) *Encyclopedia of adolescence* Garland

Brophy JE (1979) 'Teacher behavior and its effects' *Journal of Educational Psychology* 71 (6), pp733–750

Canter L (1989) 'Assertive discipline – more than names on the board and marbles in a jar' *Phi Delta Kappan* 71 (1), pp57–61

Doyle W (1983) 'Academic work' *Review of Educational Research* 53 (2), 159–200

Emmer ET, Evertson CM, Clements BS & Worsham ME (1994) *Classroom management for secondary teachers* 3rd edn Allyn & Bacon

Evertson CM, Emmer ET, Clements BS & Worsham ME (1994) *Classroom management for elementary teachers* 3rd edn Allyn & Bacon

Good TL (1982) *Classroom research: what we know and what we need to know* (R & D report no 9018) University of Texas Research & Development Center for Teacher Education

Kounin J (1970) *Discipline and group management in classrooms* Holt, Rinehart & Winston

McCaslin M & Good TL (1992) 'Compliant cognition: the misalliance of management and instructional goals in current school reform' *Educational Researcher* 21 (3), pp4–17